What Shall I Cry?

What Shall I Cry?

Kenneth G. Greet

EPWORTH PRESS

British Library Cataloguing in Publication Data

Greet, Kenneth G.
  What shall I cry?
  1. Sociology, Christian   2. Social
  history——1970–
  I. Title
  261.8'3   BT738

  ISBN 0–7162–0420–7

First published 1986
by Epworth Press, Room 195, 1 Central Buildings,
Westminster, London SW1H 9NR

Phototypeset by Input Typesetting Ltd,
and printed in Great Britain by
Richard Clay (The Chaucer Press) Ltd
Bungay, Suffolk

A voice says 'Cry', and another asks, 'What shall I cry?'
  (Isaiah 40.6)

Contents

Introduction   9

1 A Voice that Cries   12
   A duty to speak   12
   Rooted in theology   14
   Woven into history   16
   Contemporary witness   19

2 The Scandal of Poverty   24
   Pictures of poverty   24
   A global phenomenon   26
   Poverty in Britain   28
   The great divide   34

3 The Disgrace of Unemployment   39
   A tragic absurdity   40
   The church's involvement   41
   Britain's economic decline   43
   The experience of Japan   45
   Changing patterns of work   47
   The distribution of wealth   48

4 The Sin of the Arms Trade   50
   A monstrous sin   51
   Signs of repentance   52
   A big and bloody business   53
   Britain's share of the trade   55
   The nuclear arms race   57
   An American initiative   58
   Signs of hope   60

5 The Divisiveness of Privilege   64
   The Bible challenges privilege   64
   Health   67
   Education   71

6 The Iniquity of Discrimination   79
   Sex   79
   Race   86

   Notes   95

Introduction

'What shall I cry?' Every preacher is familiar with the question; it often haunts him day and night. There are many ways by which Christians witness to the truth of the gospel of Jesus Christ. It can be dramatized, set to music, made visible in the craftsmanship of architect and builder; most importantly it can and must be lived out in the details of daily life. In all these various forms of witness words play a greater or lesser part. For the preacher, however, the word is supreme. He is a voice. He is a servant of the Word of God. He is a wordsmith, always struggling to find the right words to say what he has to say, to enshrine and express the Word of God. Just what a struggle that can be is known only to those who have gone down into a dark pit of despair to mine the clear vocabulary of compelling utterance. Any fool can string words together. There is, after all, no shortage of words. But if they are carelessly chosen, and if the message to be delivered is of no consequence, the word will fall on weary ears with all the impact of sodden rags on a cement slab.

I write as a preacher. The title of this tract for the times is taken from that part of the Bible which demonstrates the preacher's role as prophet. Every preacher must be both prophet and priest. Part of his role as priest is to guard the great traditions of Christianity and in particular the story of those events which tell of God's redemptive intervention in human history. Part of his role as prophet is to proclaim the fact that the God who revealed himself in the events of long ago is equally present in the events of today.

Dr Colin Morris stresses the importance of holding in creative tension these two aspects of the preacher's task:

Undoubtedly, for many reasons, a preacher will put more emphasis on either priestly or prophetic elements in his vocation, but at all costs he must not cut the gordian knot and become either prophet or priest. For he can only speak a truly contemporaneous, prophetic word when the full burden of the historic truth of the Gospel has rested upon him, otherwise he degenerates into a commentator on current affairs. And from being a priest he will become an antiquarian unless that Faith once delivered to the

9

saints, of which he is a guardian, is constantly exposed to the gospel the world preaches to the Church.[1]

In making a Christian comment on some of the urgent issues of our time I am acutely aware of the danger of sounding like a mere 'commentator on current affairs'. The subjects which are briefly examined in the following pages are controversial. Christians do not always agree, especially on the political aspects of the matters we discuss. The fear of controversy, however, should not inhibit the prophet. He must live with the fact that if he applies the truth of the gospel to contemporary events he is likely to run into trouble. There is a long and honourable history which reflects this inescapable fact. He must also recognize that he may not always get it right. The gift of prophecy does not confer infallibility.

I do not need to be convinced about the importance of the priestly role of the preacher. For nearly fifty years I have tried not to move far from the Bible in my preaching. I have set forth the facts concerning the divine initiative whereby our salvation is secured. In season and out of season I have sought to be an evangelist offering the unsearchable riches of Christ to all who will receive them. My authority derives from the word of God set forth in the Bible. But in my comments on great public issues here I speak as prophet. If any excuse is needed for concentrating on that aspect of Christian witness it is that I believe far too much Christian preaching stops short at the crucial point where the historic revelation contained in the Bible must be related to the contemporary world. Sometimes the church and the preachers who help to shape its witness seem insufficiently aware that there is a voice which says 'Cry!'

It was that awareness which gave such dramatic urgency to the utterances of the biblical prophets. Each in his day brought the eternal word to bear on the events of his time. The Second Isaiah hears voices – prophets always do. He listens to some heavenly messenger issuing the urgent summons 'Cry!' Another voice enquires, 'What shall I cry?' The answer is that the word of our God endures for evermore (Isaiah 40.8). A voice cries, 'Prepare a road for the Lord through the wilderness' (Isaiah 40.3). Later on, John the Baptist likens himself to the prophet and asserts that he is 'a voice crying in the wilderness' (Luke 3.4).

Long years separate us from the prophets of old and yet their urgent cry often seems to have a contemporary ring. The precise historic context of their utterances differs from ours, but some of the basic issues which moved them to anger, pity and exhortation are just as surely embedded in the different situations confronting us today. One of the consistent and recurring themes of the prophets is the justice of God. It is that aspect of Christian concern that prompts the shape of what follows and the approach to the contemporary issues which I examine.

There may well be some who will complain that my chapters, brief as they must be, are long on analysis and short on solutions. I can only reply that I have not attempted to provide answers where I do not know what they should be, nor to suggest simple solutions to complex problems. But deep down I cherish two convictions. One is that the problems to which I refer, immense though they are, are not incapable of solution, given the will, the spirit and the determination to overcome them. The other conviction is that, though the prophet may not have a detailed blueprint for a brave new world, he is nonetheless under obligation to cry aloud against what is manifestly unjust.

While I am about the business of trying to forestall criticism, a word concerning the use of the masculine gender in pronouns and such references as 'mankind'. I hope that those who take strong exception to what they see as sexist language will believe that I intend no disrespect, expecially after they have read Chapter 6. The truth is that I just can't bear the disruptions to syntax and the rhythmic flow of sentences caused by having constantly to refer to both sexes or delete all words which appear to have an exclusively masculine connotation. If I have thereby caused offence to anyone, I beg to be forgiven.

Here, then, in the following pages, is a preacher's cry. Not that the chapters are in the remotest sense sermons. But they sketch in something of the social background against which the preacher must do his work. They provide material for theological reflection. As I have said, if the preacher is to be true to the prophetic tradition which is an important part of his inheritance, he must cry aloud against injustice; not injustice in general, for there is no such thing, but injustices of particular kinds in specific contexts. This he cannot do unless he immerses himself in the details of the life of the world about him. Hence the descriptive, analytical and statistical sections of the book which endeavour to make sufficiently clear what in fact I am crying out about.

First of all, however, I try, by appealing to theology and history, to establish the right and the duty of the church and its spokesmen to cry in the name of him whose love and justice are obverse and reverse of the same coin.

1 | *A Voice that Cries*

There is a voice that cries.
Prepare a road for the Lord through the wilderness (Isaiah 40.3)

Shortly after she became Prime Minister, Mrs Margaret Thatcher agreed to see a small deputation from the British Council of Churches. I opened the discussion by outlining the work of the Council and expressed the hope that channels of communication between the government and the churches would be kept wide open. I then called on my three colleagues to describe some of the work we had done on such issues as devolution and unemployment. I recall the Prime Minister's spirited response to the suggestion that the use of new technology was bound to result in loss of jobs. She pointed to all those young industries, like television, which had provided a whole range of employment opportunities. At the end of an hour Mrs Thatcher commented: 'Now you gentlemen have been talking to me all this time about social and political questions and have said nothing about the work of the churches.' I felt bound to comment that, if we had spent an hour talking about evangelism, the Prime Minister would have had every right to say, 'But have the churches no concern about the grave social and political problems with which my government has to grapple?'

A duty to speak

Since this book will be mainly about some of those problems, I had better state as clearly as I can my profound conviction that the church has both a right and a duty to speak out on the issues of the day. The exercise of that right and duty is an essential part of the work of the churches. I do not think that the Prime Minister would contest that view, however much she might dislike some of the things that some church leaders have said. There are, however, powerful voices, like that of Dr Edward Norman, which express a contrary view. He shows a somewhat dismissive attitude to 'social workers, psychologists, sociologists, educationalists, liberal windbags and chattering clergymen stuffed full of bourgeois values'.[1]

Such a critical lumping together of the representatives of various disciplines, all of whom have their own particular contribution to make to the better understanding and improvement of social conditions, reminds me of an interview many years ago with another leading politician, Lord Hailsham. Three of us, representing London churches, went to present to him the case for an increase in the British allocation to overseas aid. He told us he was rather tired of people who came begging for government money. 'It's the nurses one week and the dustmen the next, and now you,' he said. I felt it right to point out that we were not asking for anything for ourselves, and that moreover there was no such thing as 'government money': we were merely exercising our democratic right of saying how we thought our money should be distributed. At the end of the interview the noble Lord told us a sad tale about a juvenile delinquent who had committed a serious crime in the vicinity of his home. 'Don't you think,' he asked, 'you would be better employed doing your proper work in your churches and youth clubs, instead of getting involved with those other complex matters?'

The simple answer to that question was 'No'. It is not a case of 'either-or'. I think, however, that the proper Christian response to criticism must always be, first of all, to ask whether there is any element of truth in it. I recall the story recorded in II Samuel 16 of King David's attitude to a character called Shimei who showered him with stones and curses. One of the king's followers said, 'Why let this dead dog curse your majesty? I will go across and knock off his head.' But David said, 'Let him be, let him curse; for the Lord has told him to do it.'

I once heard a fine sermon preached from that text under the title 'What Christians can learn from their critics'. We should, I believe, be willing to listen to our critics, whether they come from within the Christian church, or outside it.

Let it then be readily admitted that 'chattering clergymen' and other church representatives can lay no claim to infallibility and may indeed on occasion talk the greatest nonsense. The very least that can be expected of those who make judgments on social and political questions is that they should be well briefed. There is no Christian judgment on anything in default of the facts.

It must also be recognized that there are technical matters of the greatest complexity about which only the expert is competent to speak. We must respect what William Temple called 'the autonomy of technique'. At the same time the expert must do his utmost to make the matters with which he deals intelligible to the lay person. Moreover, the expert, like all the rest of us, is accountable for the effects of the work he does and the techniques that he perfects.

Another point which needs to be made is that the church and its members may, in stressing one part of the Christian message, neglect another. Again, in its proper concern to listen to what secular man is saying, the church may neglect that which is distinctive in its own message and understanding of the world.

When all of this has been said, however, the church must challenge all who question its right and duty to speak on the great issues of the day, and also to act. That right and that duty are rooted in Christian theology and woven into Christian history.

Rooted in theology

A leading British newspaper criticized 'the interventionist antics of meddlesome clergy'. This provocative language is a pungent articulation of a heresy which, like many another Christian deviation, has had a long life. The theological basis for intervention by the Christian in the affairs of the world is that God himself has intervened. In the divine incarnation heaven and earth were joined. Jesus came 'preaching the gospel of the kingdom' (Matthew 4.23). He taught his disciples to pray 'Thy kingdom come, thy will be done, on earth as in heaven' (Matthew 5.10).

Those who dismiss what they call 'the social gospel' in favour of the gospel of personal salvation are making a division where none exists, nor can exist. There are not two gospels, but one. The gospel is both personal and social. It could not be otherwise for the obvious reason that men and women are persons-in-relationship. Remove a baby from its human environment and let it be reared by a tribe of monkeys, and that baby will not develop as a person. Humanity is the food on which I feed. The kind of person I become depends enormously on the quality of the relationships which influence me. The kind of person I am will in turn greatly affect the quality of my relationships with others. I cannot become a person on my own. Even the solitary monk in his cell is not exempt from this fundamental fact of human existence. His first experience of love was in the close contact with his mother experienced in the womb where his short tenancy was initiated by an act of love between two people. Doubtless he was led to his vocation by the influence of others who helped to mould his convictions. His cell is the place where he communes with

God and through his prayers and reading relates to innumerable people whom he never sees.

Some of the manifold implications of this understanding of personhood and how it is created are explored in Dr Jack Dominian's book *The Capacity to Love.* He says: 'the symbol of the body of Christ as representing the community of Christians developed by Paul means indubitably that the image of God in man is always to be found in relationships of love, that between man and God extended between "I" and "thou" in community'.[2]

Although man's constitution as a 'being-in-relationship' is clearly established by psychological and sociological exploration of his nature, for the Christian it is most significantly set forth in the assertion that he is made in the image of God (Genesis 1.26). The image of God is trinitarian: within the Godhead are three persons in relationship with each other. This profound statement of what, in the nature of the case, must be an ineffable mystery, may well evoke the response: 'I just don't understand what it means.' Of course no-one comprehends all that it means, and it would be intolerable arrogance to pretend otherwise. That need not prevent our taking firm hold of the bits of the doctrine that we are capable of understanding. One important truth that is enshrined in this basic statement about God may be expressed thus: God can only be God in the context of community, and the men and women he has made can only be human within that same context.

The implications of this for the mission of the church are far-reaching. Any suggestion that evangelism is concerned only with the conversion of the individual makes no sort of sense, either theologically, psychologically or sociologically. Any change in the heart of the individual is bound to affect the network of relationships which are part of what he is.

But conversely, changes in the community of which he is a part will affect the individual. Christian mission, therefore, must be concerned both with personal conversion and with changing the structures of society.

It is an inescapable fact that sin gets itself organized. Opposition to sin is bound, therefore, to bring Christians into conflict with structures and institutions which are inimical to human welfare. To plead that religion be kept separate from politics makes no more sense than suggesting that breathing and living be isolated from each other.

St Paul, who has a way of stating the purposes of God in language which is as compelling as it is comprehensive, declares that through

Christ 'God chose to reconcile the whole universe to himself, making peace through the shedding of his blood on the cross – to reconcile all things, whether on earth or heaven, through him alone' (Colossians 1.20). The 'all things' to which he refers include thrones, sovereignties, authorities and power (1.15,16).

So the apostle shows how the role of the Old Testament prophet is taken up into the ministry of Christ and his church. Redemption is offered by the prophets, but always on the other side of repentance, and that change of mind must be both personal and corporate. Amos portrays a God who is sickened by religious observance unrelated to social rectitude: 'Spare me the sound of your songs; I cannot endure the music of your lutes. Let justice roll on like a river and righteousness like an ever-flowing stream' (Amos 5.23, 24). The sort of sins against which the prophet protests in the name of the Lord are these: 'For crime after crime of Israel I will grant them no reprieve, because they sell the innocent for a pair of shoes. They grind the heads of the poor into the earth and thrust the humble out of their way' (Amos 2.6,7).

It all sounds startlingly contemporary. The resolutions of church assemblies about oppression in Latin America and the deprivations suffered by workers in South Africa may be couched in more innocuous language than that used by Amos, who was a master of inspired invective, but the message is the same.

Woven into history

If, then, the right and the duty of the church to speak out on the great issues of the day are rooted in Christian theology, they are also woven into Christian history. Stanley G. Evans made a brave attempt to survey the social aspects of religious faith down the ages, beginning with the Old Testament and the teaching of Jesus about the kingdom, examining the theory and practice of the mediaeval church, the fluctuations in Christian social teaching, and the modern attempts to address the pressing problems of a deeply divided world. Towards the end of his review he has an important passage about the Christian sacraments:

What all the sacraments proclaim is the Christian view of the interpenetration of spiritual and material. The tragedy of life is division: the goal of life is unity. The sacraments assert the unity of spiritual and material, for life is whole; they assert the unity of aspiration and fulfilment; they assert the unity of man with man;

they assert the unity of man with God. The sacraments enact and proclaim what Christian doctrine asserts, that good is not an abstraction but something which has to be made incarnate, that truth and peace and justice and all that is desirable are not phrases to be mouthed but realities to assert and realities which have to be worked out in the entire order of human society and expressed in material terms.[3]

It is this sacramental sense of 'the interpenetration of spiritual and material' which again and again has informed and inspired the witness of the church.

If through lack of space I am compelled to choose just one illustrative snippet of history, then I must turn to the Methodist tradition in which I stand. For seventeen years I served as secretary of what is now the Division of Social Responsibility of the Methodist Church: a department which has twice changed its name to indicate an ever-expanding remit. I was very conscious of standing in an interventionist tradition going back to Wesley himself and beyond him into the scriptures, of which he was a faithful exponent.

No man can be removed from his context in history, but it is interesting to speculate on the sort of thing that John Wesley would be saying about the social evils of our day. He was a great pamphleteer and crusader. We may dip into the voluminous literature he produced to find a few examples of his trenchant attack on those things which he found offensive because they were blatant contradictions of the Christian ethic as he understood and taught it.

We may begin with slavery. The great institution of slavery which Wesley attacked has largely disappeared, but it exists in subtler though often quite dramatic forms. What, one wonders, would Wesley make of package tours which include the provision of oriental prostitutes *en route*? Certainly in his own day the 'execrable villainy' of slavery, as he called it in the last letter he wrote (to William Wilberforce), weighed heavily on his mind. Even on his death-bed he asked that passages be read from the autobiography of a black slave which had greatly impressed him. His own *Thoughts upon Slavery* was published in 1774. 'Are not stubbornness, cunning, pilfering and divers other vices the natural and necessary fruits of slavery?', he asks. To the slave merchants he says: 'You know that your slaves are procured by means nothing near so innocent as picking of pockets, house-breaking or robbery on the highway . . . You are the spring that puts all the rest in motion – captains, slave owners, kidnappers, murderers . . . Thy hands, thy bed, thy furniture, thy house, thy lands are at present stained with blood.'

He calls on Christians to work for the suppression of this evil traffic:

> Give liberty to whom liberty is due, that is to every child of man, to every partaker of human nature. Let none serve you but by his own act and deed, by his own voluntary choice. Away with all whips, all chains, all compulsion. Be gentle towards all men.

No less direct were Wesley's condemnations of war. In 1776 he published a *Seasonable Address to the More Serious Part of the Inhabitants of Great Britain respecting the Unhappy Contest between us and our American Brethren*. He describes the armies on both sides thus:

> But what are they going to do? To shoot each other through the head or heart, to stab and butcher each other? . . . Why so? What harm have they done to each other? Why none at all. Most of them are entire strangers to each other. But a matter is in dispute relative to the mode of taxation. So these country-men, children of the same parents, are to *murder* each other with all possible haste – to *prove* who is in the right. What an argument is this! What a method of proof! What an amazing way of deciding controversies! . . . Are there no wise men among us? None that are able to judge between *brethren*? But brother goeth to war against brother, and that in the very sight of the heathen. Surely this is a sore evil among us? How is wisdom perished from the wise! What a flood of folly and madness has broke in upon us!

One more example of Wesley's understanding and outspoken espousal of the social implications of Christian faith may be taken from his utterances on wealth and privilege. If the great evangelist failed to address the radical causes of injustice and inequalities in society as many Christians try to do today, at least his teaching on the stewardship of money was plain and direct. In a sermon entitled *The Good Steward* he refers to 'that precious talent which contains all the rest – money'.

But money must never be an end in itself.

> In what manner didst thou employ that comprehensive talent, money? Not in gratifying the desire of the flesh, the desire of the eye or the pride of life? Not squandering it away in vain expenses, the same as throwing it into the sea? Not hoarding it up to leave

behind thee, the same as burying it in the earth? But in first supplying thine own reasonable wants, together with those of thy family; then restoring the remainder to God, through the poor?

Certainly Wesley lived out his own precepts regarding wealth. He earned a great deal of money from his writings but lived on £30 a year. In one period of twelve months he gave away £1,400. When in 1776 he received a letter from the Commissioners of Excise suggesting that he was in possession of plate that he had failed to declare, he made a brief reply: 'I have two silver spoons at London and two at Bristol. This is all the plate I have at present, and I shall not buy any more while so many round me want bread.'

Contemporary witness

The church must speak out. The phrase is familiar enough, and I have argued in support of it, showing that the right and duty of the church, both to speak and act, is rooted in theology and woven into history. But who speaks for the church and how is the voice of the church to be effectively heard?

The brief paragraph I have just written moves from what appears to be a stark and simple point stated in a single sentence to a question which immediately opens up issues of considerable complexity.

It would appear at first sight that the Roman Catholic church has found and embodied the simplest answer to the question. The Pope speaks for the church and what he says is bounced around the world on the sounding-board of the media which the Vatican uses with impressive, not to say expensive, effectiveness. I had a brief opportunity of examining this remarkable system more closely when, following his historic visit to Britain, the Pope invited a small group of us from the British Council of Churches to spend a week in the Vatican. The power of the Pope is not absolute, but it is considerable. He is, of course, advised by the representatives of the various departments of the Curia. He is subject to many pressures. But his personal authority was evident from the way in which, again and again in conversations within the various Vatican offices, the Holy Father was quoted. I talked with one of his speech-writers who revealed that often the Pope will himself redraft whole sections of a prepared speech before he is satisfied with it.

The Roman Catholic system has both strengths and weaknesses. Its obvious strength is the acceptance by a global community of massive numerical strength of a series of well-articulated teachings on moral and social questions. Part of the weakness of the system is that it makes it difficult for the church to change its position when change is required. The Roman Catholic church sometimes looks like one of those gigantic oil tankers which take twelve miles of deceleration before they can stop and go into reverse. So increasingly there is rebellion among those who find some of the teaching unacceptable. When the Pope reiterates the traditional ban on 'artificial' methods of birth control, he looks very much like King Canute with the tide lapping over his red shoes. The teaching of Pope John Paul II on the temporary acceptance of the doctrine of nuclear deterrence is not accepted by numbers of faithful Catholics.

What of the Protestant part of the Christian church, divided as it is into so many different denominations? Is not the Protestant witness rendered useless by the fact that there is no one who can speak for the whole and also that the separate parts often speak with a divided voice?

There can be no doubt that division means weakness. That is one reason why so many Christians care deeply about the promotion of unity among the followers of Christ. But the situation is not without its encouraging aspects. More and more the churches are learning to study the great issues of the day together. This is done at the world level through the World Council of Churches, and at the national level through national councils of churches. Roman Catholic participation in these conciliar efforts is increasing all the time.

I recall a fascinating and prophetic piece of work undertaken by a BCC working party over which I presided. Its report entitled *Human Reproduction: A Study of Emergent Problems and Questions in the Light of the Christian Faith* (1962) was the result of inter-church co-operation and the use of a variety of experts. We examined the experiments which were far advanced in the world of animal husbandry and which before long might become capable of human application. In fact events have moved more rapidly than we then supposed. We tried to indicate the moral and theological questions that would be raised by such techniques as the use of host wombs, the induction of multiple births, and sex selection (the last of these lying still on the horizon). It was a good example of the churches pooling their resources and seeking together to anticipate and confront 'future shock', to use the title of Alvin Toffler's striking book.[4]

Two perennial problems confront the churches as they seek to make an informed and effective social witness. They are the problems of internal and external communication. Much of the excellent work done by ecumenical working parties never gets down to those who at the local level must bear the Christian standard. More resources need to be put into this essential bridge-building task. Similarly with media communications, the churches are too slow to recognize the importance of using press, radio and television effectively.

Inevitably the representatives of the media turn to those from whom they can expect an immediate and intelligent response to matters of moment. In England the established church has a built-in advantage in that its principal officers, the bishops, occupy a recognizable, if not always a well-understood, place in the life of the nation. This advantage can, of course, turn out to be a liability when a particular bishop happens to be the kind of character who never opens his mouth without putting his foot in it. The Church of England, however, through its Press and Information Service, takes the problem of communication seriously. Of the English Free Churches, the Methodist Church is the only one to employ a full-time press officer. The fact that the titular leaders of the Free Churches change annually means that they are not in office long enough to establish effective relations with the media. The same applies to the Moderator of the Free Church Federal Council. Plainly many of these difficulties would be greatly modified if the British churches came together in a single body. In the meantime there is need for more effective back-up of those who, whether by reason of office or of natural leadership abilities, are points of reference for the news men and the broadcasters.

The Archbishop of York, recognizing that the church cannot speak with a single voice, urges the need for church leaders to create the kind of environment within which prophetic voices can be heard.

> This means giving space and encouragement to those who actually know about the matter in hand and can speak out of their own direct experience. It is a fact that much of the new life in the Churches arises, not from the top, but from individuals and groups and those with some special interest, who catch a vision and pursue it and eventually manage to share it. Top-heavy initiatives, on the other hand, often cause resentment and resistance, especially when they derive too obviously from the supposed need felt by leaders to be seen to 'do something'.[5]

This is a wise reminder of the many different ways in which the voice of the church may be heard.

There is another point that must be made about the right and duty of the church to speak out on contemporary issues. Politics is the art of the possible and inevitably involves compromise. Many Christians talk as if compromise is always and inevitably an evil thing. They speak of 'the need for moral absolutes', forgetful of the fact that it has often been those who hold inflexibly to absolutist notions who have inflicted extremist measures and much suffering on those who refused to conform. This is how I put the matter in a book which tried to summarize much of the experience of working for seventeen years in the Social Responsibility Division of the Methodist Church:

> On matters such as the law on Sunday or the law controlling gambling, Christians are apt to hold views different from those of other sections of the community. If the government introduces a measure of which Christians do not approve or cannot wholly support, they can indicate their outright opposition. There may be occasions when this is the only proper course to take. More often, however, the Churches will enter into discussions designed to secure such amendments as may improve the Bill if only to the extent of modifying its more objectionable clauses. If this is thought of in terms of compromise, then it must be said that it is the sort of compromise which Christians must be prepared to accept as necessary to the exercise of responsible citizenship.[6]

In an appendix to the volume already quoted, the Archbishop of York argues that there is a middle ground between moral absolutism and weak indecisiveness which the Christian can legitimately occupy. I believe this to be true, but the Christian must always find that middle ground uncomfortable. He must be concerned to define the limits of acceptable compromise.

Recognizing the limitations of all human endeavours he will nevertheless maintain his conviction that bad situations can be improved. He will also be aware that there are times when the will of God is clear and his demand unequivocal, though the attempt to respond faithfully may involve costly suffering.

In the light of all this, what should be the relationship of church to government? In Romans 13 St Paul puts a high value on the institutions of government: 'Every person must submit to the supreme authorities. There is no authority but by act of God, and the existing authorities are instituted by him; consequently anyone who rebels against authority is resisting a divine institution' (Romans 13.1,2). If this sounds like a rather too thorough endorsement of the authority of the state, it must be remembered that Paul knew all about the faults of government: he himself was wrongfully imprisoned; he knew that the state crucified Jesus. The command to be submissive cannot be absolute, for the state itself can promote evil. Civil disobedience is a biblical concept. We are required to obey the state only up to the point where to obey would be disobedience to God.

If we examine the social witness of the church today, it is clear that there is one dominant issue which unites millions of Christians in a fellowship of conviction and protest. It is the issue of justice in a world where division is everywhere causing strife and endangering the whole life of mankind. The WCC holds before the churches the goal of creating 'a just, sustainable and participatory society'. But the world is not like that: poverty festers in the shadow of prosperity; the greed of man pollutes the environment so that in many places life itself can hardly be sustained; and millions suffer from a sense of powerlessness leading to despair. It might be possible to bear some of the manifestations of injustice if it were clear that things are improving. But in many areas there is no such assurance.

In Britain, whilst the general principle of the church standing in 'critical solidarity' with government is accepted by Christians, there has been an increasing emphasis on the need for a critical response to government policies. The reason for this is that many of those policies result in the rich growing richer while, by comparison, the poor grow poorer. The consequence is that the fabric of society is disrupted by violence and the sense of injustice grows stronger. It is with some of the manifestations of this injustice that we shall be concerned in the chapters that follow. To the Christians of today, as to the prophets of old, 'a voice says "Cry", and another asks, "What shall I cry?" ' It is with that question that we must be concerned.

2 | *The Scandal of Poverty*

They grind the heads of the poor into the earth
and thrust the humble out of their way (Amos 2.6)

God loves all his children. But that does not mean that he exercises a benign neutrality in his dealings with the world in which they live. The Bishop of Liverpool has argued that there is a divine bias for the poor.[1] It is a fact to which the Bible repeatedly testifies. In the Old Testament the prophets take up the cudgels on behalf of the poor and against the rich who oppress them. Deuteronomy states: 'There will never be any poor among you if only you obey the Lord your God by carefully keeping these commandments which I lay upon you this day' (Deuteronomy 15.4). This is a word to the whole community. If there is poverty, the blame is shared by all: they have contravened the will of God. Not only does Jesus pronounce special blessing on the poor (Luke 6.20), he says that he has been sent 'to announce good news to the poor' (Luke 4.18), and he emphasizes the perils of riches: 'It is easier for a camel to pass through the eye of a needle than for a rich man to enter the Kingdom of God' (Mark 10.25).

Increasingly the scandal of poverty is troubling the conscience of right-thinking people. Cocooned as most of us are in comparative affluence, it is nevertheless impossible to escape from the fact that vast numbers of people live in conditions of appalling deprivation. Famine in Africa has been vividly portrayed on our television screens, and public response in terms of generous giving has been impressive. But with growing awareness there has come also a dawning recognition that the problem of poverty is more complex than many have realized.

Pictures of poverty

I have tried before writing this chapter to recapture some of those personal experiences which have left their mark on my mind as I have encountered the sight, the sound and the smell of poverty. Here are three such experiences.

Years ago I visited Abyssinia. The Emperor Haile Selassie was still on the throne, and he invited me to dinner at the royal palace. It was a scrumptious banquet served on gold plates. The Emperor moved among us, short of stature, but the very quintessence of royal dignity. He was a Christian believer and would stop his car to fling coins to the beggars who lined the highway. A member of his household said to me: 'It won't last much longer, you know. This whole set-up is doomed.' She was right. An educated Ethiopian said caustically: 'The Emperor's great achievement is to have dragged his country out of the thirteenth into the fourteenth century.' I still recall vividly the distress I felt at the sight of so much abject poverty and near-starvation, somehow magnified by the contrasting experience in the imperial palace.

In Haiti I visited an area called La Saline. It is a bog on which the poorest of the poor have built crude shanty dwellings constructed of bits of rusty tin sheeting and cardboard. It is not difficult to sink over your ankles in green slime. There is no proper sanitation. The local rubbish tip is infested with rats; lean pigs and bedraggled hens scratch for odd scraps of food. I entered one of the houses, a single room containing the ruins of a bed. An old man was making some sort of a meal for his bed-ridden wife. She stretched out a skinny hand to greet me. I can still hear the hacking cough that convulsed her frail body: one of the sounds of poverty.

There is the smell, too. As a small boy I went every Thursday evening with my father to a downtown Band of Hope meeting in the centre of Bristol. The Band of Hope was dedicated to teaching the virtues of total abstinence to the children of the poor parents, many of whom found their only escape from the intolerable slums in drinking away their meagre resources. My father played the piano for the odd assortment of entertainers who were waiting to enter the battle-lines. They were sometimes pelted with improvised missiles, the most offensive being small glass phials called 'stink bombs'. These added a sulphuric flavour to the already foetid atmosphere. Poverty can have a rank and rotten smell.

The reason why I have taken space to paint these pictures is an important one. When we talk about poverty we are talking about people. It is easy to keep the discussion at the level of cold statistics and to examine schemes and strategies in a rather detached and academic way. True, the scandal of poverty needs careful analysis, but it requires also passionate concern and commitment, for the poor are our sisters and brothers, often without a voice and without hope. Most important of all, they are people for whom Christ died and for whom he had a special regard.

A global phenomenon

The pictures of poverty I have just painted are taken from scenes at home and abroad and are, perhaps, a sufficient reminder of an obvious fact: that poverty is a global phenomenon. That fact is only one of many which have combined to drive home upon us the recognition that the world we inhabit has become a 'global village'. Such observances as 'One World Week' have helped to fill out this concept. Many writers have elaborated on the theme of our interdependence in a world where it is now clear that the only viable unit of survival is the human race. One of the most notable exponents of this thesis was the late Barbara Ward. She brought to her task immense knowledge and a visionary enthusiasm which was infectious.

I recall her addressing the Lambeth Conference of Anglican bishops and preaching a kind of secular ecumenism which was a profound challenge to the churches to recognise the implications of what God is doing in calling them to leave behind the irrelevancies of denominational divisions. In *Only One Earth* Barbara Ward speaks movingly of our essential environmental interdependence:

> Our links of blood and history, our sense of shared culture and achievement, our traditions, our faiths are all precious and enrich the world with the variety of scale and function required for every vital ecosystem. But we have lacked a wider rationale of unity. Our prophets have sought it. Our poets have dreamed of it. But it is only in our own day that astronomers, physicists, geologists, chemists, biologists, anthropologists, ethnologists and archaeologists have all combined in a single witness of advanced science to tell us that, in every alphabet of our being, we do indeed belong to a single system, powered by a single energy, manifesting a fundamental unity under all its variations, depending for its survival on the balance and health of the total system.

> If this vision of unity – which is not a vision only but a hard and inescapable scientific fact – can become part of the common insight of all the inhabitants of Planet Earth, then we may find that, beyond all our inevitable pluralisms, we can achieve just enough unity of purpose to build a human world.[2]

This book was followed by *The Home of Man*, in which the shift from rural to urban life is examined. In this century the percentage of world population living in cities will rise from one-sixth to over one-half. Once again the author shares her global vision. The increasing dialogue about the great world-wide problems of poverty, hunger and environmental pollution could signal the growth of a new loyalty, not to old divisive nationalisms, but to common membership of the human family.

The book ends with a question and a plea:

Too vast a dream? Too naive a hope? Perhaps – yet we can now talk to the ends of the earth as easily as villagers once conversed with each other. Our planetary interdependence is as great as that of earlier states. Our knowledge is world-wide. Our airs and oceans are equally shared. So are all the preconditions of material existence. If man has learned to be loyal to his nation as well as to his family and his town, do we have to argue that no further extension of loyalty is possible – to the planet itself which carries our earthly life and all the means of sustaining it?

This is perhaps the ultimate implication of the underlying unity of scientific law first discerned by the Greeks, of the underlying law of moral brotherhood and obligation most passionately proclaimed by the Hebrew prophets. Today they come together in a new fusion of vision and energy to remind us of our inescapable unity even as we stand on the very verge of potential annihilation. The scientist and the sage, the man of learning and the poet, the mathematician and the saint repeat to the human city the same plea and the same warning: 'We must love each other or we must die.'[3]

In *Progress for a Small Planet* Barbara Ward describes the crisis facing the world as a result of pollution, the prodigal consumption of raw materials many of which are irreplaceable, and the strains between rich and poor. The conclusion reached is this:

The only fundamentally unsolved problem in this unsteady inter-regnum between imperial ages which may be dying and a planetary society which struggles to be born is whether the rich and fortunate are imaginative enough and the resentful and underprivileged poor patient enough to begin to establish a true foundation of better sharing, fuller co-operation, and joint planetary work. . . . No problem is insoluble in the creation of a balanced and conserving planet save humanity itself. Can it reach in time the vision of joint survival? Can its inescapable physical interdependence – the chief new insight of our century – induce that vision? We do not know. We have the duty to hope.[4]

I have given some space to the testimony of Barbara Ward because she articulated so clearly a message that is being preached by the representatives of a variety of secular disciplines. It would be a scandal if the churches failed to hear the message and were not deeply involved in the exploration of the implications of all this for the Christian mission in the world.

I want now briefly to examine the situation in Britain and then to look at the wider question of the North/South divide, remembering always that poverty is a global fact and that what happens in one part of the world can have vital consequences in other parts of the world.

Poverty in Britain

There are many in Britain who assume that in our country at any rate we have got rid of poverty. They might read my account of inner-city poverty in the Bristol of fifty years ago and say, 'all that, thank goodness, is a thing of the past'. Others take the view that if there are poor members of our society today, it must be their own fault, the result of laziness, irresponsibility or sheer incompetence. Neither of these views will stand up to honest examination.

It is true that most people in Britain today are better off materially than they would have been fifty years ago. It is undeniable that the situation of some is damaged by laziness, irresponsibility and incompetence. The fact remains, however, that large numbers of people are poor through no fault of their own. It is also true that their number is growing. They measure their poverty by comparing their lot with that of the more favoured members of the community.

It is often stated that poverty and riches are comparative terms, and that, of course, is true. If I compare my own situation with that of an Ethiopian peasant, then I recognize that I am wealthy. I never go hungry, I lack nothing, I have virtually no financial anxieties. If, however, I compare my financial resources with those of certain television performers who earn in a week more than my pension provides in a year, then I will be reckoned poor. It's all a matter of comparison. The newspaper on my desk announces that Lord Gowrie is retiring from politics because he can't live on his ministerial salary of £33,000 a year. Clearly, there can be no absolute standard by which poverty is assessed; it must be judged on relative criteria, by comparison with the standard of living of other groups in the community. Accepting that as inevitable, what is the current situation in Britain?

Those who brought the welfare state to birth dreamed great dreams. It was to provide for the basic needs of all those whose living-standard fell below 'the poverty line'. This line was to be continually adjusted in the light of the economic situation of the country. No one would be allowed to fall through the safety net thus created. In fact there were always those who fell through the net. They were the unfortunate members of the community: the handicapped in mind and body, the victims of family breakdown and the social misfits. Now the ranks of the poor are swollen by the unemployed school-leavers, the victims of redundancy and economic recession, the one-parent families and the homeless. Many of these poor members of our society are trapped in areas of urban decay where squalid housing conditions, lack of facilities and general drabness lead to family breakdown and the violence of increasing rebellion.

A great deal of research has been undertaken by the Child Poverty Action Group. It states:

There is no official definition of poverty and there are many different ways of measuring it.

Supplementary benefit (SB) is supposed to provide a 'safety-net', that is, a minimum level of income for those not in full-time work. For this reason, the supplementary benefit scale rates – which are approved by Parliament – tend to be treated as a poverty line, although the government itself denies that there is such a thing.

Because the supplementary benefit rates are so low, a slightly broader definition of poverty is often used. Households with incomes slightly higher than supplementary benefit are also considered to be poor or living on the margins of poverty. Government figures (see below) describe as 'low income' all those living on incomes up to 140% of their supplementary benefit entitlement.

Many studies have shown that the money provided by supplementary benefit is inadequate and the annual reports of the government's advisory body have pressed for increases in the spending power of the rates. CPAG's own research has come to the same conclusion.[5]

In 1982 the average weekly expenditure, excluding housing costs, of couples with two children was £134.05. For a two-child family living on supplementary benefit the rate was £61.80, less than half the average. Such families suffer real hardship. They cannot afford adequate heating, must rely on cheap clothing, and often have to miss a meal. They are debarred from any satisfying participation in the life of the community.

Government figures for 1981 show that 15 million people were living on low incomes (defined as up to 140% of supplementary benefit level). Of these, 7.7 million were living on or below the supplementary benefit poverty line. The total number of people dependent on supplementary benefit has increased dramatically. In December 1981 there were 6.1 million. By August 1983 this had become 7.2 million.

A particularly distressing fact is the changing age of the poor. In 1979 just over half of all those living below the poverty line were pensioners and just over a quarter were living in families with children. Two years later the proportions had changed to 36% and 38% respectively.

The lot of many of those caught in the poverty-trap is worsened by their failure to claim the benefits to which they are entitled. In 1981 – the latest date for which figures are available – only 71% of those eligible claimed supplementary benefit, roughly the same percentage claimed rent rebates, 65% claimed rate rebates, and in 1978–9 only 51% claimed family income supplement. In 1981 £760 million of supplementary benefit went unclaimed. There are several reasons for this failure to claim what is due. Benefits are means-tested, and many people do not like having to show that they have a low income. Others miss out because they are unaware of their rights and the DHSS has not done enough to put the information around. The number of staff dealing with claims for supplementary benefit has been significantly reduced, which is plain daft at a time when those claims are multiplying.

The government's tax policy has increased rather than alleviated the problem of poverty. Many poor families find that if their wages rise they pay more in tax and national insurance contributions but lose some or all of their means-tested benefits, such as family income supplement, free school meals and housing benefits. In effect, the government is giving with one hand and taking away with another. Although there has been wide support for the proposal to increase child benefit, it remains at a quite inadequate level. Moreover, since the late 1950s the real level of tax-free income received by families with children has fallen, while at the same time that enjoyed by the childless has risen.

How are the churches reacting to this rising tide of poverty in Britain? There is, of course, still far too much evidence of complacency and ignorance. On the whole the church in Britain is a middle-class institution full of respectable people who know little at first hand of what poverty means. They admire the Salvation Army for undertaking the smelly end of the church's mission, but are very thankful that the sort of conditions described by William Booth in *In Darkest England and the Way Out* now lie a century behind us. But there are also encouraging signs of an awakened conscience and a deepened awareness. The Methodist Church describe its 'Mission Alongside the Poor' programme as, among other things, 'a learning project'. If it is abundantly clear that death and destruction on the streets of Soweto are due to the manifest injustices of an evil system, it is increasingly recognized that the horrible scenes in Brixton, Toxteth and Handsworth are the result of evils that lie deep in the structures of our own society. In Handsworth, for example, half the young adults are unemployed and up to 80% of black youth have no work. In spite of the statement about spending £20 million in recent years on housing improvements made at the time of the riots in September 1985, still many of the dismal houses have no inside toilet. Such a combination of circumstances is a passport to chaos.

It is important in commenting on the unrest in our inner cities to try to distinguish between explanation and exculpation. When houses are burnt to the ground, shops destroyed and looted, and innocent people murdered, it is right to describe these as criminal acts. But to describe the Handsworth riots, as did the Home Secretary, as 'criminality, pure and simple' is to betray an insensitivity and indeed a 'naïvety', to use a word somewhat over-employed by government spokesmen, which are almost unbelievable. The statement of the Birmingham District Synod of the Methodist Church, issued shortly after the event, reveals a much greater grasp of the inescapable realities of the situation. The statement refers sympathetically to the difficulties confronting the police and to the fact that many factors combined to precipitate the troubles, but it continues: 'We believe the underlying causes lie in feelings of hopelessness and alienation due to long-term unemployment and social neglect. Many in the community feel rejected and voiceless, and have lost confidence in the democratic processes.'

In their attempt to understand and redress the problem of poverty, the churches need to examine carefully the underlying factors of recession, industrial, cultural and economic changes, and the effects of modern technology. But there is also the more immediate requirement critically to assess government policies. The Director of the William Temple Foundation has commented on both these tasks in a lecture delivered to the Oxford Institute for Church and Society.[6] He gives four main reasons for rejecting the policies of the Conservative government. The first is that those policies are making a bad situation worse. The plight of the vulnerable is increasingly desperate. Secondly, some of the policies actually produce poverty. An example is the advocacy of low pay as a way of combating unemployment. The result is that many move from unearned poverty to earned poverty. Thirdly, the Government is requiring the more vulnerable members of the community, rather than the advantaged, to bear the cost of economic change. The following passage makes the point:

> It may be that the Government will have to tell the nation that we must pass through a time of tribulation during which there will be general reductions of living standards. If these are to be borne by everyone – the well-off as well as the poor – then it may be acceptable that social security beneficiaries, protected by some assured minimum safety net, should bear their share of the trouble too. But to say that the rich must receive generous tax deductions and that pay and pensions must be index-linked, while the poorest and politically weakest members of the community should bear cuts in living standards which richer people are to be spared – that is morally indefensible.[7]

The fourth reason for rejecting Government policies is that they reflect a too uncritical and doctrinaire acceptance of the philosophy of the market economy. This approach was strongly criticized in the Bishop of Durham's maiden speech to the General Synod of the Church of England in November 1984:

> If acting on monetarist principles steadily increases the number of the poor and makes the rich even richer it must be challenged. It is no answer to say: 'But this is the only way forward . . .' This is as dogmatic as the claims of Marxist Socialism about the necessity of the party to promote the good of the people so that bureaucratic inefficiency and totalitarian violence are both necessary and justified . . . The costs of any policy are part of the grounds for judging it, and possibly of opposing it. A faith about economics or about politics which insists that all sorts of social costs and

personal sufferings are justified now because we are surely right, the world is like this, and this is the only realistic programme, is a false faith, in fact verging on idolatry.[8]

In the second half of his lecture John Atherton tackles the longer-term task of sketching out the sort of thinking that is needed for the construction of feasible alternatives. He seeks to set this thinking within a Christian theological framework. His first line of thought recognizes the importance of not relying exclusively on any one ideal economic type. He advocates the introduction of what is called 'the impurity principle'. In reading his development of this idea I was reminded of a fascinating lecture to which I listened during a recent visit to China. It was delivered by a leading Chinese economist. His central thesis was that the use of the impurity principle was essential to the development of a successful and balanced economy. 'If you try out a theory and it doesn't work,' he declared, 'then, however good the theory, it must be discarded and some other approach tried.'

The second line of thinking advanced by John Atherton concerns a wider view of society, and the need for a reformulation of the common good. This line of approach stresses the importance of interdependence and dialogue and the avoidance of the extremism that results from over-dependence on either the concept of the market economy or of state planning.

Returning now to the more immediate critique of government policies, I must refer again to the excellent work done by the Child Poverty Action Group founded in 1965. It campaigns for four major objectives:

1. If supplementary benefit is to be the 'safety net' for the few, and not for millions of people as now, national insurance benefits must be set at a rate higher than supplementary benefit and the rate must genuinely meet people's needs. It must provide for all those unable to support themselves through paid employment, irrespective of the number of national insurance contributions people have paid.

2. Child benefit needs to be increased substantially to help families with children, in particular working families. At the moment it is less than the amounts provided for children through the supplementary benefit and long-term national insurance schemes. Child benefit could be almost doubled at no extra cost to the country if the married man's tax allowance was abolished (at 1983/4 rates). In the long term, there should be one *adequate* benefit for all children, paid

regardless of whether the parent is in work or out of work. This would also be a major simplification.

3. A national minimum wage must play an essential part in any programme to tackle low pay.

4. Government figures show that since 1979 tax cuts have benefited the better off far more than those on low incomes, let alone those who have incomes so low that they don't pay taxes. But, to get rid of poverty, resources need to be redistributed from the well-off to the poor. A start could be made by making better use of the large sums of money spent on some tax reliefs – often described as the 'hidden welfare state'– for the better-off.[9]

The amount of poverty in Britain has increased in almost the same degree as the growth in unemployment. There can be no solution which does not tackle the curse of joblessness. That daunting prospect is examined in the next chapter.

The great divide

I must now return to the point made earlier that poverty is a global phenomenon. When I use the word 'must' I am referring to a fact which, for the Christian, is inescapable. It was because 'God so loved *the world* that he gave his only Son' (John 3.16). Membership of the church is incorporation in a world-wide family. As Bishop Newbigin has said: 'We dare not talk of welfare as though it were a matter simply of these islands off the coast of the Eurasian continent. We are part of one world. Welfare as Christians think of it can only be the welfare of the whole human family.'[10]

In looking at the situation of the poor in Britain we have found ourselves contemplating that most dreadful of human conditions, hopelessness. Where there is hope there is life, but without hope life is really not worth living. There is the hopelessness of the victims of poverty, and there is also the hopelessness of those who would like to do something about it but are overwhelmed by the immensity of the problem. I must therefore at this point include a simple word of testimony. Some people seem able to maintain a chirpy optimism in the face of everything, presumably either because of some quirk of temperament or because they wear blinkers which effectively prevent their seeing things as they really are. A Christian is required to face the facts. There is no way in which the meeting of that requirement can be made to sustain a chirpy optimism. There is really no ground for human optimism. Christian hope is different. It is not escapism, neither is it a self-generating attitude of mind. It is quite simply (and

34

very profoundly) a gift of God. It is the ability to persevere with the most difficult tasks without losing heart, believing that the important thing is not to win the next battle but to be fighting on God's side in a war that *he* can't possibly lose.

It was necessary to take firm hold of this basic article of faith before looking at the facts about world poverty because they are daunting. If in Britain rich and poor seem to live in two different nations, their counterparts in the global village seem to inhabit different worlds. The rich nations of the world live mainly in the North and the poor in the South. The gross disparity between them was admirably summarized in the Brandt Report:

The nations of the South see themselves as sharing a common predicament. Their solidarity in global negotiations stems from the awareness of being dependent on the North, and unequal with it; and a great many of them are bound together by their colonial experience. The North including Eastern Europe has a quarter of the world's population and four-fifths of its income; the South including China has three billion people – three quarters of the world's population but living on one-fifth of the world's income. In the North the average person can expect to live for more than seventy years; he or she will rarely be hungry, and will be educated at least up to secondary level. In the countries of the South the great majority of people have a life expectancy of close to fifty years; in the poorest countries one out of every four children dies before the age of five; one-fifth or more of all the people in the South suffer from hunger and malnutrition; 50% have no chance to become literate.

Behind these differences lies the fundamental inequality of economic strength. It is not just that the North is so much richer than the South. Over 90% of the world's manufacturing industry is in the North. Most patents and new technology are the property of multinational corporations of the North, which conduct a large share of world investment and world trade in raw materials and manufactures. Because of this economic power Northern countries dominate the international economic system – its rules and regulations, and its international institutions of trade, money and finance. Some developing countries have swum against this tide, taking the opportunities which exist and overcoming many obstacles; but most of them find the currents too strong for them. In the world as in nations, economic forces left entirely to themselves tend to produce growing inequality. Within nations public policy has to protect the weaker partners. The time has come to apply this precept to relations between nations within the world community.[11]

Herr Brandt in his Introduction to the report says:

Situations are seldom hopeless if they are not accepted as such. And hope itself is the most important element in overcoming obstacles which might otherwise seem insurmountable.[12]

Here is the statesman turned preacher. He is pleading for a change in attitude or, if you like, for conversion. Nothing less will do.

The Brandt Report examines all the interrelated problems which, taken together, threaten the whole future of the race. They include poverty, hunger, population growth, squandering of resources on arms, reckless use of raw materials, environmental pollution, unjust economic systems and sheer ignorance. On all these matters recommendations are made which, if heeded, could begin to turn back the tide of disaster that threatens the human family. Here are voices that cry. How far are they being heeded?

Certainly it can be said that, so far as the churches are concerned, the educational work has been developing apace. The needs of the poor countries are increasingly understood, and such vital questions as the connection between disarmament and development (highlighted in the Brandt Report) are constantly discussed. Agencies like Christian Aid, through their accumulated experience in the field, speak with increasing authority. Inevitably, and rightly, they find themselves involved in politics. This often brings them into conflict with the Charity Commissioners, but how can such involvement be avoided? It is often easier to collect money than to ensure its most effective use. The work of aid and development is hampered by political arrangements which perpetuate injustice, inefficiency and corruption.

Oxfam's 'Hungry for Change' campaign is an excellent example of a nationwide educational campaign aimed at informing people about facts and bringing pressure to bear on members of parliament. The campaign concentrates on three particular issues.

The first of these is trade. Most developing countries depend on a small range of exports. For example, 70% of Zambia's exports are copper. Price fixing is largely done in commodity markets, particularly in New York and London. Prices for exports have been falling while at the same time the prices of consumer goods which the poor exporting countries need have been rising. The price of cocoa, for example, on which Ghana so much depends, fell from £1500 per ton in 1980 to £900 per ton in 1982. I saw some of the disastrous effects of this on a visit to Ghana where the shadow of economic decline was deepening.

Another example of how the precarious economy of a poor country can be threatened is the arrangement which ensures a good price to EEC farmers for sugar beet. This is dumped on the world market at a low price and poor sugar-producing countries are forced to sell their produce at less than it costs to produce it.

There are no easy answers to the question posed by these facts. The UN plan to establish a Common Fund to help finance agreements fixing production quotas deserves support. Britain was, in fact, one of the first countries to agree to this plan. The developing countries must play their part in seeking to tackle the problems created by unfair trading arrangements. Little good will be done if the result of improved revenues is merely further to line the pockets of the millionaires who are to be found even in the poorest countries.

The second issue in the Oxfam campaign concerns the debt crisis. Many poor countries repay more in debt charges than they receive in new loans. The African countries south of the Sahara, which are presently the focus of so much concern, have debts in excess of $80,000 million. They must pay $11,000 million in interest charges and capital repayment. This just about cancels out what they receive in aid. Britain, to her credit, has cancelled repayment from some of the poorest countries. Some poor countries borrow from the International Monetary Fund to help them repay their debts. But this only increases their problems. The IMF imposes harsh conditions, such as cutting back on government expenditure, and thus the lot of the poor is worsened.

Britain is in a good position to urge other countries to write off the official debts of the fifty poorest countries.

Thirdly, there is the question of aid. The UN has set an aid target of nought point seven percent of Gross National Product. But Britain's aid is only half of this: the 1983 figure was 0.35%. The comparable figures for other countries were: France 0.76%, Germany 0.49%, Norway 1.06% and USA 0.24. The British government responded to the needs of the Ethiopian famine victims, but the money sent was taken out of the existing aid budget and merely transferred from development to relief.

There is great need for the creation of stocks of non-perishable food for rapid use in emergency conditions. The kind of aid given is also important. It is needed, of course, for the building of railroads and similar projects, but even more for those services that directly help the poorest of the poor, like the provision of health care and clean water supplies.

The cry of the poor is indeed the sound of a voice crying in the wilderness – a wilderness of misery, squalor and deprivation. But it is a wilderness that can be made to blossom as the rose. If we are clever enough to land a man on the moon, there can't be any of the technical problems relating to the abolition of poverty that can't be solved. What is needed is the will and the passion to see justice prevail. There is hope in the stirring of conscience the world over and in the recognition that the world is a unity: we stand or fall together. The cry of the oppressed is answered by the prophetic cry of those who combine to address the centres of power and demand that justice be done.

3 | *The Disgrace of Unemployment*

Our economic system was not created by God . . . and what man has
created man can change (Tony Benn)

Immediately after my ordination the Methodist Church sent me to
the Tonypandy Mission in the Rhondda Valley in South Wales. A
couple of weeks before I was due to begin my ministry there I went
down to look over the place. My predecessor, Dr Cyril Gwyther,
took me to the Central Hall and the first thing I saw was a line of
unemployed men leaning up against the wall at the front of the
building. 'You will see,' he said with wry humour, 'that the Central
Hall is well-supported.' Descending to the lower part of the premises
I discovered a small army of women serving cheap lunches to a crowd
of poor people. Later on, when I came to know and love the people
who lived in the rows of mean houses arranged like ranks of dominoes
along the steep slopes of the Valley, I learned much about the
suffering of the 1930s when more than half of the men of the
community were without work. The Methodist Mission sought to
relieve the physical needs of the poor and to minister to their souls.
Much of the creative activity of those days was pioneered by another
of my predecessors, the Rev. R. J. Barker, a man of great vision and
remarkable gifts: poet, preacher, politician, thinker and musician.

By the time I began my seven-year sojourn in the Rhondda Valley
much of the travail of those dire days of depression was a distant
memory to those who had experienced it. When I got to know the
unemployed men who leaned against the wall of the church I
discovered that they were victims of silicosis, the miner's disease
which hardens the lungs and makes breathing painful. I have seen
many a man die of that disease. But with the gradual shutting down
of the collieries many of the younger people had left the Valley to
seek employment elsewhere. Those still employed in the mines were
better off than they had ever been. The general view was that the
1930s were an unhappy chapter in a past that would never be
repeated.

A tragic absurdity

That optimism was unjustified. It is true that history never repeats itself. The new poverty caused by unemployment today is different from the old, as Jeremy Seabrook argues so forcefully. Contrasting the sense of community among the poor of an earlier day with the bitterness and lack of a sense of purpose among many of today's unemployed he says:

> The 'creation of wealth'has become an almost mystical obsession, and it has come to constitute the sole matter of all political debate. One observable result of this in all working-class communities has been a disruption, discontinuity in the old ties, the old associations, the bonds of kinship, neighbourhood and workplace, without any serious political resistance. The enormous forfeits which have been exacted as a condition of material advance have been separated from it, neutralized, disconnected from the process of which they are an integral part. In this way the exaltation of things has deeply damaged the care for people.[1]

The fact that unemployment is spiritually damaging is a sufficient reason for deep concern, especially among Christians. But unemployment on a vast scale is also an enormous absurdity. Wherever one looks there is work to be done. The public services complain of shortage of staff. Customers often have to wait in queues in post offices because more than half the counters are unattended, school classes are overcrowded and hospitals do not have sufficient nurses. If you complain to the Inland Revenue office that it has taken them three months to answer a letter, they tell you that they are grossly understaffed. Many people have to live in appalling houses which cry out for renovation or replacement. Yet between three and four million of our people, most of whom are eager for a job, are kept in idleness. It makes no sense at all.

This co-existence of unmet needs and unused human energy makes even less sense when the cost of it is considered. Something of the cost in terms of human frustration and despair among the unemployed people themselves has already been mentioned. But we all share in the cost. In financial terms, taking into account loss of taxes and national insurance contributions, the cost to the nation of each person on the dole is about £7000 annually: more than £20 billion in all. This staggering amount is contributed by the taxes largely paid by those in work.

Why is this extraordinary state of affairs allowed to continue?

How has it come about? What can and should be done about it? Representatives of government point to the measures taken to alleviate the problem, like youth training schemes and job-creation programmes. None of these measures, however, has prevented the unemployment figures from soaring still higher.

Quite clearly, no government wants to see unemployment increasing. No party is likely to win an election on the slogan 'See how the number of jobless has increased while we have been in office'. Obviously, then, unemployment is an intractable problem and there are no slick answers to it. It is, however, entirely right to ask whether the problem is not, at least in part, the consequence of pursuing the wrong policies. If so, are there alternative policies which would produce better results in spite of Mrs Thatcher's repeated assertion that 'there is no other way'?

The church's involvement

These are important questions. Should the church be involved in the search for answers, and are there special insights from Christian faith that will assist the search? Or is the proper Christian attitude the one which says: 'These political questions should be left to the politicians and the experts in economic theory; they are in any case highly complex, so our responsibility a is a pastoral one: we must try to understand the feelings of the unemployed and minister to them, hoping in the meantime that something will turn up'?

Beyond all doubt the church has a pastoral responsibility for the unemployed, as indeed it has for the employed. Many of those who are holding down well-paid jobs suffer from stress or because of discrimination and injustice. But the needs of the unemployed must be of special concern to a caring church. Those needs will not go away, for there are no immediate solutions to the problems which give rise to them. The situation has in fact been growing steadily worse. However, to suggest that such a caring pastoral ministry exhausts the church's responsibility is to deny that there is a distinctive contribution to be made to the long-term remedy of a situation which has become intolerable.

The British churches have indicated their involvement in the task of analysis and political debate on long-term solutions in a number of reports. There is an encouraging degree of agreement on a number of basic points. One such report, the product of inter-Divisional cooperation, was presented to the Methodist Conference in 1983.[2] The report alludes briefly to the past fifty years and to the continuing

41

debate between neo-classical theory, of which monetarism is an expression, and Keynsian theory. The former holds that the market system is inherently efficient and self-adjusting provided it is left to itself, whereas the the latter argues that there is no reason why the market system should achieve equilibrium without intervention. During the 1950s and early 1960s the economic management of the country was based on an attempted synthesis of these two theories. The Government sought to maintain employment levels by fixing interest rates, taxes and public expenditure at appropriate levels, to control inflation and maintain a healthy balance of payments. Investment policies, structural and technological development within industry, however, were left to the market.

The mid–1960s saw a change in these priorities. The balance of payments rather than the level of unemployment became the measure of good economic management. By 1968 there were half a million unemployed. By 1972 the number had doubled. World economies were seriously affected by the dramatic rise in oil prices in 1973. The inflation rate in Britain rose to more than 25% in 1975. Mrs Thatcher took office as Prime Minister in 1979. The key factor in her policy was the reduction of inflation by control of the money supply. By the beginning of 1983 inflation had fallen to well below 10% but unemployment had risen to well over three million.

Britain's situation cannot, of course, be viewed in isolation from that of the rest of the world. International prosperity is very largely determined by that of the 'top ten' industrial nations, of which Britain is one. When the Western nations reacted to the increases in the price of oil by cutting back on imports from one another and on supplies of raw materials from the Third World they shifted the burden of balance of payment deficits onto the weaker nations. This led to a long-term recession.

Having reviewed the present situation and its background, the Methodist report makes the following judgment:

The Christian community has a prophetic responsibility to interpret the present crisis in the light of its understanding of the character and purpose of God, to bring to the debate the values and insights of the Gospel, and to proclaim a message of judgment and hope. If there is to be a turning away from crisis then the true nature of the crisis must be recognized and the judgments accepted.

Twice in the twentieth century crises associated with economic depression have been arrested by war – in 1914 and in 1939. In neither case was the war the solution to these crises. War was not a turning point: it was a detour. The structures, values and goals of the market economy have remained fundamentally unchanged and crisis has recurred.

The technological revolution, which has major implications for social, political and economic structure, is a *potential turning-point*. However, technology is not neutral: like economics, it reflects and reinforces power-structures and value systems. Technological revolution provides a context for change: crisis provides the imperative.[3]

The report then goes on to make important points, echoed in other church statements, about the way people are valued and work is understood. Far too often people are valued only because of the work they do. The unemployed person is poorly regarded because he has no paid job. This evaluation in economic terms only is a denial of the gospel which teaches that people matter as people because they matter to God. Certain kinds of employment can be degrading, while voluntary unpaid work can be satisfying, useful, and enobling. After all, the largest category of such work is that done by the housewife, or home-maker as some prefer to be called: an essential vocation in which vast numbers have found creative satisfaction and fulfilment. 'A society ordered primarily to serve the ends of the market economy . . . usurps the sovereignty of God.'[4]

Critical comments such as these, valid as I believe them to be, should not obscure the fact that the creation of wealth is a proper and legitimate exercise. Indeed it is altogether essential when one considers the ends it must serve. The pursuit of wealth for its own sake is to be condemned. But if the aim is to create an efficient industrial base in order to underwrite the cost of more effective social services, educational facilities and so on, then Christian conscience can only approve, provided always that the methods used are also consistent with Christian principles.

Britain's economic decline

The problem of massive unemployment is not peculiar to Britain. In the European Economic Community there are more than twelve million unemployed, which is nearly 12% of the labour force. In Britain and France one in four young people under twenty-five is out of work and of those two-fifths have been jobless for more than a year. We have to recognize, however, that in many ways Britain is economically backward and, though the fact is partly disguised, behind our present troubles lies a long history of industrial decline.

At the end of the last century Britain was the workshop of the world and was able to draw on the vast resources of a global empire. The situation is altogether different now. The Empire no longer exists, and we have many competitors. We import more manufactured goods than we export. Between 1970 and 1980 our manufacturing labour force was reduced from 7.9 million to 6.9 million. In the five years since 1980 a further 1.75 million jobs have been lost, while week after week brings news of factories closing, and large areas which once were scenes of intense activity are now an industrial wasteland littered with the rusty remains of unused and outmoded machinery. Although in 1984 some 250,000 new jobs were created, many of these were part-time and were taken by women workers not counted in the normal unemployment statistics. The rise in the number of jobless continued. It is now reckoned that one-third of those without work will be without a job for a long period. About 300,000 a month lose or take up a job; this change of job process takes an average of about eight months. Altogether one in eight of the working population is unemployed. But among young people under twenty-five the rate is one in four if they are white, and one in two if they are black.

It must be remembered that Britain's decline has continued in spite of the boon of North Sea oil. The value of that resource will, however, now begin to decline. Tax revenues reached a peak last year (1985) of about £12,000 million. By 1990, allowing for the possible expoitation of new fields, that figure will be reduced to £8,000 million, and by the end of the century the great oil bonanza will be practically over. Shirley Williams makes the following critical judgment on Britain's use of this liquid asset:

Britain will have little new investment in manufacturing or in the basic structures of its economy to show for its sudden wealth, no upsurge of education, no marked improvement in the skills of its work-force. In the tradition of the imperial power it once was, Britain has invested its oil revenues abroad. Dividends from those investments will enrich the City of London and help to finance a rapidly worsening balance of trade. They will not be providing jobs for unemployed Britons, nor re-equipping manufacturers to export, nor upgrading men and women with outdated skills or no skills at all. The oil revenues have been squandered on tax-cuts for the well-off and on investments overseas, neither of which are likely to assure the country's future.[5]

The Central Advisory Council for Science and Technology was set up in 1967 to advise the Government on the ways in which the best use could be made of our scientific and technological resources. Its report, *Technological Innovation in Britain,* exposed the weakness of a country which has failed to keep up with technological innovations and to invest sufficiently in prototype work, production and marketing. The report also draws attention to the inadequate emphasis within our educational system on the need for engineers. Japan, for example, with a population roughly twice the size of that of the United Kingdom, has an annual output of young engineers exceeding 70,000. The UK produces about 16,000, and a quarter of them are overseas students. The Finniston Report of 1980, *Engineering our Future,* stressed the same point.

If industrial decline, lack of innovative enterprise and weakness in our educational system resulting from a cultural bias in favour of the arts rather than the sciences are contributory factors in our economic weakness, another is the a sustained saga of poor industrial relations – 'the English disease'. It is easy enough when examining particular damaging disputes to apportion blame between management and unions. Both sides need to make great changes in traditional attitudes. The key to success is the recognition that there will be benefits for both labour and management if confrontational tactics are abandoned in favour of consultation and cooperation.

The experience of Japan

Many commentators have compared Britain's situation with that of Japan. Japan's postwar economic recovery is a remarkable success story. Between 1960 and 1978 her national income grew by more than 8% per year. Whilst it would be unwise to assume that everything that works well in Japan could profitably be transferred to this country, it is impossible to overlook the fact that our situation has many parallels with hers. Both countries are comparatively small overcrowded islands. Both have to rely on imported food and raw materials. Both are heavily dependent for their national income on export success.

One vital factor in the Japanese story is her willingness to make use of the fruits of the modern technological revolution. A fascinating example of this is the widespread use of robots in Japanese factories:

45

40,000 in the automobile industry alone (the 1982 figure). Robots are being manufactured at a tremendous rate and their price is falling – by as much as 30% in 1983. Consider the economic attractiveness of an arc-welding robot which can be purchased for roughly twice the amount that a skilled worker will earn in a year. The robot can work all night as well as all day and will probably 'earn' for the factory about three times as much as a man working on the same production line. The introduction of new types of robot continues and in their performance they more and more resemble that of human intelligence applied to the job in hand. It will be possible to send robots into dangerous environments, thus removing some of the human hazards which attend certain kinds of work such as the maintenance of nuclear power plants. There is a story of a computerized factory which employed just one man and a dog. The dog guarded the factory and the man fed the dog. The story is apocryphal but it caricatures the sort of developments that will increasingly change the face of industry.

But even more important than the new technologies is the attitude of cooperation between management and labour that characterizes much of Japanese industry. The unions insist on full consultation and keep under careful review the effects of introducing microelectronics. Although the use of new technology inevitably results in a smaller labour force, virtually full employment has been maintained by very large increases in output and sales.

Japan is not without its problems. Older workers do not find it so easy to adapt to the new technologies as the younger ones. The ratio of female to male workers has declined because those who qualify as scientists and engineers are overwhelmingly male. In a great many cases workers who are unable to hold down the new highly technical jobs are retrained for other work.

There is, however, still much argument among observers of Japan's phenomenal economic success as to exactly how this has been achieved. There are also some who believe that this success has involved unacceptable social costs. The diversion of resources into industry has resulted in quite inadequate social service provisions and in major problems of pollution. It is only fair to note that Japan's industrial success has been built on the basis of a poor society that lacked the kind of welfare services that we have taken for granted for many years past. One point is beyond dispute: government planning and coordination of policy through the Ministry of International Trade and Industry (MITI) has had an enormous effect. Keith Smith makes the following perceptive comment:

Consensus cannot be achieved without a framework of discussion, debate and bargaining in which goals are worked out and methods of achieving them agreed. Japanese industry certainly has such a framework in MITI; but it also has powerful policy instruments to generate growth, and this in itself is likely to promote consensus.

Japanese consensus, therefore, may not be so much a cause of its growth record, as an effect of an economic policy which is recognized to have widespread benefits.[6]

There may be much that Britain could learn from the Japanese recovery.

Changing patterns of work

If the rejuvenation of our economy and the generation of wealth require a much greater willingness to introduce advanced technology, the question we have to face is the one the BCC delegation attempted to discuss with the Prime Minister in the interview referred to at the start of Chapter 1. The new techniques of automatic control of machinery destroy old methods of production and change the patterns of work. In the twenty-five years between 1948 and 1974 the labour force in agriculture and forestry declined from 786,000 to 415,000; in fishing from 37,700 to 12,200; in coal-mining from 802,700 to 314,000; in railways from 695,000 to 224,000; in ports and docks from 155,700 to 81,500; in textiles from 928,500 to 596,700. In all those areas reductions have continued. If, however, we consider the service industries, we see a very different picture. During the same quarter of a century the labour force rose in food, drink and tobacco from 646,500 to 783,900; in air transport from 32,100 to 79,800; in post office and telecommunications from 353,200 to 509,700; in distribution from 2,167,900 to 2,810,100; in insurance, banking and finance from 425,900 to 680,500; in health from 525,900 to 1,175,200; in education and local government from 1,280,500 to 2,752,400.[7]

A moment's pondering of these figures will reveal how great are the changes they reflect. In general the trends they indicate towards increasing employment in the 'tertiary sector' have continued, though, of course, the immense growth in clerical work is bound to be affected by the introduction of computers and other labour-saving technology. But clearly the service industries provide enormous opportunities for employment, so long as sufficient wealth is created to enable us to pay for them.

Another factor in the changes to the work pattern is the increase

47

in the number of women in paid employment: now about 40% of the total work force. Rather more than half of that 40% are full-time and the rest are part-time.

In spite of the evidence that new technology creates many new jobs it is an inescapable fact that its overall effect is to reduce the size of the labour force required, or at any rate the number of working hours needed, to maintain adequate production. How is this situation to be dealt with?

If the introduction of high technology results in the production of more wealth, then obviously the number of working hours can be reduced without affecting the general standard of living. Britain's record in this regard compares unfavourably with that of some other countries. In this country in 1980 the average hours worked in a week were forty-four compared with forty-two in West Germany, forty-one in Holland, forty and seven-tenths in Japan and thirty-five and eight-tenths in Belgium.

Of course, the prospect of shorter working hours, including the growth of the opportunities for leisure and for earlier retirement raise profoundly important questions about how time is to be profitably used and indeed life itself organized. These questions are surely of the greatest significance to the church, concerned as it must be with the ultimate meaning and purpose of human existence.

The distribution of wealth

Another issue which in the long term will be of the greatest importance is that of how wealth will be distributed in the high technology society we are creating. At the end of an admirable essay on the issues we have been considering Bishop E. R. Wickham comments as follows:

Income for most people is derived from their work, in wages and salaries. How will income be derived in the high technology society? Somehow, income, spending power, corresponding to the wealth generated by society, will have to be distributed across the nation, and personal income, for considerable years of life, will not be directly derived from one's work. The nexus, that is to say, between work and income will be weakened, and even snapped. But this is also a process already at work in our society, even if incipiently and inadequately . . . through pensions, family allowances, education grants, social security benefits, and so on. At present there may be restraints on this development through our economic failures, and no doubt there will always be restraints and limits of some kind, but it is impossible to believe that we have reached the end of the process. We have usually seen these things as part of a welfare state. We must begin to see them – and further developments – as the inevitable logic of the high technology society. It is axiomatic that the economic and social ordering of society should reflect the level of technology that has been reached, and we need more public debate on how wealth should be distributed in the high technology society, in ways that are realistic and not simply utopian. That must be regarded as a fundamental moral issue. Already ideas and models exist in such concepts as the 'social wage', the 'social dividend', the 'guaranteed annual income', 'negative income tax', and the concept of social security itself. If some of the terms are new – though some of them have been about for a quarter of a century – the core of these ideas has a very long history, going back to the nineteenth century, the seventeenth century or the fourteenth century, all periods that saw Europe in economic travail, into the centuries of biblical prophecy. Only today does technology begin to promise their realization. And the term 'unemployment', dare we say, with all its miserable associations, might be thrown into the dust-bin of history.[8]

As Dr Wickham acknowledges, such long-term thinking provides no immediate solution to the problem of unemployment. It is nevertheless important to ensure that we are moving in the right direction. There can be no such assurance unless there is some agreement about the goals we seek and the means whereby they are to be realized. The church, with its dedication to the creation of 'a just, sustainable and participatory society', must contribute fully to the debate about how we can move forward towards that end. The goad that drives us on is the deep awareness that in spite of real progress in some areas of our national life, injustice persists. On 24 October 1985 the Prince of Wales expressed his concern about conditions in the inner cities – areas of high unemployment. He was reported as stating privately that he did not want to become king of a divided nation. Inevitably he was criticized by some for appearing to interfere in politics. But the heir to the throne was right to respond to the cry that goes up from those who are the victims of the kind of injustice that is endemic in the structures of a society that condemns so many to worklessness and, all too often, to a sense of worthlessness.

4 | *The Sin of the Arms Trade*

The guns spell money's ultimate reason (Stephen Spender)

It is quite impossible for a Christian to talk sensibly about the way things are in the world without referring to sin. The word means disobedience to the will of God, and the world is full of evidence of just such disobedience.

The inclusion of the word in the title of this chapter is quite deliberate. There are many things that can be said about the international arms trade. It aids and abets one of the most monstrous myths ever to infect and enslave the minds of men, namely that you can render the world safe by making it ever more unsafe. The adage 'if you want peace, prepare for war' still exercises its malign influence on the architects of national security. The blind following of this fundamental principle of militarism has brought the human race to the point where the possibility of global extermination is discussed *ad nauseam* simply because, for the first time in history, it is a real possibility.

Not only is the arms trade a destabilizing factor in the modern world, it is economically debilitating. It does, of course, provide employment for millions of people and the fact that it does so is sometimes advanced as an argument in its favour. But investment in this nefarious trade is dead-end investment. The same degree of investment in peaceful industries would produce far more jobs and end-products which could greatly benefit mankind. The fact is that the arms trade is unbelievably wasteful. Vast quantities of armaments are produced at prodigious cost, only to be declared obsolete before they have been used. What would be the general judgment on an automobile factory that manufactured millions of motor cars and consigned them all while they were still new and unused to an enormous scrapheap? It would be regarded as economic madness on a monumental scale. But this is precisely the kind of mind-numbing stupidity which characterizes a large part of the arms trade.

I shall examine some aspects of the arms trade more closely later in this chapter. Before I do so, however, I must come to the major charge which is that what we are talking about is a monstrous sin. It is no answer to that charge to say that nations must be provided with the means of protecting a themselves from the assaults of their enemies. That is not a consideration that noticably motivates the vendors of military hardware. Moreover, many of the armaments of today are of such potential destructive power that former distinctions between offence and defence have lost any meaning they may have had. The Trident system of so-called defence which Britain proposes to introduce in place of Polaris, which is rapidly becoming 'obsolete', is a first-strike weapon. We are actually invited to consider a scenario in which it would be considered right, however regrettable, to obliterate millions of people to 'defend ourselves' against an offensive not yet launched. There is a name for this gross distortion both of language and of moral concepts: it is sin, and the church has a right and a duty to say so.

But the sinfulness of the trade and the policies which control it (or is it the trade which determines the policies?) is reflected most vividly in the appalling misdirection of resources which are desperately needed by the poor and underprivileged. While millions exist on the edge of starvation, lacking the basic necessities of life, ever-increasing sums of money, ever-expanding resources of scientific inventiveness and human energy, are used to create the engines of death. Weaponry manufactured by wealthy nations is sold for profit to poor nations many of which use the hardware they have imported to repress the starving citizens who would rebel, if only they had the strength.

Of course, the whole miserable business is clothed with the garments of pseudo-respectability. Armaments manufacturers speak of their trade as being the same as any other. Knighthoods have been awarded to some of the most successful traders. Moreover, the public affairs of nations are conducted within a military framework which many accept without question. Uniforms and martial music and the memories of battles long ago are all part of the panoply of the nation state. Governments expend huge resources on trying to ensure the defence of the realm against 'the enemy' (who the enemy is depends on which chapter of the history book you happen to be reading), and seem scarcely to give a thought to the vital question of how enemies can be changed into friends. And this in spite of the fact that clearly it can be done and it has happened. Britain fought France in every one of the last nine centuries until the present one, but today the two countries are united by close ties of friendship and common interest. Though they have differences of opinion it is unthinkable that they should ever go to war over them.

Only one thing can save the world from disaster and that is conversion, by which I mean a radical change in the way we approach the business of living together in the global village within which the only viable unit of survival is the human race. There is no conversion without repentance. And there can be no repentance without an acknowledgment of sin.

Signs of repentance

There are signs that repentance is growing. The fact that the rejection of the outrage of nuclear weaponry is often most manifest among some who are strangers to the religious experience and language familiar to Christians should be an enormous challenge to those who profess the name of Christ.

I recognize that indignation is a reaction in which Christians should indulge only sparingly. Far too many resolutions of church assemblies begin with the words 'we deplore'. But there are some matters about which Christians do well to be angry; indeed if they are not stirred to anger by them, there is something defective about the conscience which is prepared to acquiesce. If ever there was a reason for righteous wrath, it is to be found in the evil with which this chapter is concerned. What other response can there be to a loathsome trade that feeds the fires of human aggressiveness, makes profits out of degradation and misery, and provides the death-carts in which humanity could yet hurtle to destruction?

I want, then, to belong to a church that has fire in its belly, that protests with prophetic anger against the sin of the trade in arms. Anger, however, is not enough. There must be disciplined argument based on factual information and a deep concern to find effective ways of controlling a machine that often seems to have run completely out of control. There is a place for the preaching that kindles the fire of righteous anger. Indeed, unless there is a deep a conviction of sin, a clear recognition that we are dealing with an evil that has to be opposed, we shall not have the will to struggle against what are, in fact, titanic adversaries. Fiery rhetoric can play its proper part in calling men and women to action, but the translation of conviction into effective programmes and policies requires knowledge of the facts and clear thinking.

A big and bloody business

Let us take a closer look at the arms trade. I was invited to tour a very large armaments factory in the USA. The official who conducted me round the place was an urbane character who was obviously proud of the establishment he helped to run. I asked him, 'Do you ever produce any new types of weapon here?' He laughed and said, 'I have hundreds of research workers engaged on nothing else. Yes, we are proud to claim that we have pioneered a number of original techniques.' He might have been talking about new and improved toasters or food-mixers. 'Why do you have always to be producing new weapons?' I asked. My guide stopped and, with evident surprise at so naive a question, said, 'Well, my dear fellow, it's the only way to stay in business.'

At least it was an honest answer, but it provided me with a first-hand glimpse of what the late President Eisenhower called 'the power of the industrial/military complex' with its inbuilt and demonic momentum. The production and sale of arms is big business. It is also bloody business. With the weapons it produces the antagonists in some hundred and fifty wars during the last forty years have killed perhaps twenty million people. I am not arguing that the armaments kings caused the wars, but they made them possible and often exacerbated the tensions that led to open conflict. Of course, those involved in the business try to pretend that their real concern is for peace: they are only providing the means of deterring attack and preserving stability. But the real situation is more accurately reflected in the comment of Frank S. Jonas, an agent for Remington: 'We certainly are in a hell of a business when a fellow has to wish for trouble so as to make a living.'

One of the consequences of the international trade in arms is that often weapons sold abroad are turned against the countries which have manufactured and sold them. In the First World War British guns sold to Turkey were fired against British soldiers at the Dardanelles. During the Battle of Jutland both sides used shells with Krupp fuses. In spite of the pretence that arms are sold to friendly countries, the boomerang of destructiveness strikes again and again, because, of course, friendly nations do not always remain friendly; and also, arms purchased by one nation are often sold to another.

Little wonder, then, that when the leaders of the victorious allies met at the end of the First World War they loudly condemned the arms traders. Woodrow Wilson inspired the inclusion in the Covenant of the League of Nations of the statement: 'the Members of the League agree that the manufacture of munitions and implements of war is open to grave objections'. It was, however, a pious assertion. Export of arms continued, with Britain in the lead.

The coming of peace brought problems for the arms trade, and firms like Vickers and Armstrong's tried to convert their manufacturing capacity to motor cars, railway engines and a whole range of other products. During the 1930s there was a strong movement of public opinion against the trade. Typical of the attack was an article in 1934 in *Fortune* magazine. It stated that in the First World War it had cost $25,000 to kill a soldier 'of which a great part went into the pocket of the armament maker'. Public resentment at the profits derived from human misery spread from the USA to Britain and resulted in the setting up of the Royal Commission of 1935. Those who spoke in defence of the trade made much of the point that the export of arms was a constant incentive to efficiency and innovation and brought technological advantages through the 'spin-off' into other industries. The Commission's report, whilst recognizing the special dangers inherent in the trade, nevertheless concluded that the 'reasons for maintaining the private industry outweigh those for its abolition'.

The increasing threat of war in the late 1930s changed public opinion, and the British firms dealing in arms had soon recovered from the recession. The manufacture of guns, ships and now aircraft provided work for large numbers of those who had been unemployed. Criticism of the trade was forgotten by all but a few.

As the Second World War continued the weaponry pouring from the factories became ever more complex and expensive. The emphasis increasingly was on a combination of light industry and advanced science. Governments became more and more involved in the business of weapons production and research. Leadership in the arms trade passed from Britain to the two super-powers, the USA and the USSR. Nevertheless in the decade following the war Britain sold vast quantities of arms: over 2 billion dollars' worth to private traders and 1.7 billion's worth to foreign governments. These figures do not include warships, of which during the same period Britain provided ten for the Middle East, twenty-six for Asia and Australia and five for Africa. France also developed her armaments industry in a spirit of ruthless competition. But neither Britain nor France could rival the USA and became increasingly dependent on her for advanced technology.

The deep involvement of governments in arms production and exports conferred a new respectability on the trade. While governments talked much about disarmament and peace they continued aggressively to exploit the commercial opportunities afforded by the export of arms. So in 1966 we find Denis Healey indulging in a typical piece of political hypocrisy. He said in the House of Commons:

> While the Government attach the highest importance to making progress in the field of arms control and disarmament, we must also take what practical steps we can to ensure that this country does not fail to secure its rightful share of this valuable commercial market.

Mr Healey later announced the creation of a new post in the Ministry of Defence, that of Head of Defence Sales.

In the 1960s there was intense debate about Britain's policy regarding the export of arms to South Africa. In 1963 the UN, conscious of universal opposition to the Republic's apartheid policy, called on member states to cease selling arms to South Africa. The British Conservative Government abstained when the vote was taken. However, when Harold Wilson came to power the following year he announced a full embargo on arms for South Africa, though in fact by various devices military equipment continued to get through.

With the steady disintegration of the British Empire, more and more of our former dependencies became autonomous states. As such they sought to establish their credentials before the world. Regrettably, if inevitably, they adopted the symbols of power of the rich nations and built up their military strength. A new and expanding market for the arms dealers of East and West opened up and the scene was set for the super-powers to fight their wars by proxy on other peoples' territories.

Britain's share of the trade

Britain continues to play her part in arming the nations of the Third World. More than three-quarters of her sales are to those nations, many of whom cannot manage to feed their own peoples. At the Ministry of Defence in Whitehall there is a permanent exhibition of British weapons to which potential customers are taken. It is beautifully laid out and there are models indicating how the weapons operate when the war game is played. There is no blood anywhere, of course, and nothing to offend the susceptibilities of the eminently respectable people whom it is hoped will be seduced by the shining hardware on display. There is a section devoted to what some call 'repressive technology' and other 'misguided idealists' have been known to describe as 'instruments of torture'.

The October issue of the *Newsletter of the Campaign Against the Arms Trade* gives details of major export orders during September 1985. The following items reflect something of the range of British involvement:

A deal with Saudi Arabia estimated to be worth £4,000 million.

A deal with Jordan worth £270 million.

Agreements to sell up to £100 million worth of military equipment to Egypt.

A sale of Sea Harrier jump-jets and missiles to India worth £160 million.

A sale of air-defence radar systems to Oman worth £40 million.

News that quantities of military equipment were sent to Iran – the first country in the world to denounce the UN Declaration of Human Rights.

During the 1970s a spate of evidence emerged regarding the extent to which bribery and corruption had become an integral part of the trade. In the USA a Senate committee chaired by Senator Frank Church unearthed startling information. One of the most scandalous revelations was that the firm of Lockheed had paid a million dollars to Prince Bernhard of the Netherlands in connection with an arms deal. The Dutch Prime Minister appointed a committee of investigation which discovered a record of shady dealings. The prince was compelled to resign all his public positions. This was only one instance of a network of corrupt practices implicating the arms industry in scandals affecting the political life and stability of countries around the world.

It is one of the ironies of recent history that Japan, which played its ignominious part in the Second World War has, as we saw in the previous chapter, achieved astonishing prosperity without being involved in the sale of arms. The post-war constitution of Japan states that 'the Japanese people forever renounce war as a sovereign right of the nation and the threat or use of force as a means of settling international disputes'. In 1977 the British Ministry of Defence sent a ship, the *Lyness,* on a cruise through East Asia. It was a travelling arms exhibition full of guns, missiles and other military equipment. The Mayor of Tokyo refused to allow the ship to enter the port. The shadow of Hiroshima and Nagasaki, the cities destroyed by the

American atom bombs dropped in 1945, still haunts the minds of Japanese people.

The nuclear arms race

During the years since those dread events, which changed the course of history and the nature of warfare, superimposed on the traffic in so-called conventional arms has been the appalling build-up of the nuclear arsenals of the world. During the 1950s the nations moved away from the concept of 'general and complete disarmament' to that of arms control. But the fruits of endless discussion have been meagre. When President Kennedy presented the Partial Test Ban Treaty to the American people in 1963 he recalled a a Chinese proverb and described the treaty as 'the first step on a journey of a thousand miles'. However, it is arguable that the limited arms control agreements so far secured have actually inhibited attempts to bring about real disarmament. We still await what is desperately needed: a comprehensive test ban treaty. There are children being born on the islands of the Pacific so grossly deformed by the effects of radiation from nuclear tests that they are called 'the jellyfish babies'.

Some of the agreements which have been reached relate to a promise not to do things which it is unlikely anyone would wish to do. An example is the Sea-Bed Treaty of 1972 which agreed not to place nuclear weapons on the sea-bed. One commentator described this as being as fatuous as an agreement not to bolt your aircraft to the runway. There have also been agreements not to do what at the time could not be done. The major example of this is the 1967 Outer Space Treaty which contains a pledge that space shall not be militarized.

Another agreement which has proved dangerously defective is the Non-Proliferation Treaty of 1967. It demanded no real sacrifice from the existing nuclear powers but was regarded, rightly, as discriminatory by many of the non-nuclear countries. A number of countries with nuclear potential simply refused to sign. These include Argentina, Pakistan, Brazil, India, Israel and South Africa. The nuclear powers have not fulfilled their obligation under Clause 6 to begin the process of disarmament.

Since 1969 there have been two sets of lengthy and complex negotiations on arms control between the super-powers, known as the Strategic Arms Limitation Talks. The SALT 1 talks led to a treaty which restricted each side to two sites for the deployment of anti-ballistic missile systems and an interim agreement limiting the numbers of launchers and delivery systems to those currently deployed. In fact it was only an agreement to do what both sides intended anyhow. The hope that this would be followed by a comprehensive treaty on offensive weapons (SALT 2) has not materialized.

It is instructive to note that the term 'nuclear arms race' is a literal description of the course of events since the end of the Second World War. The USA produced the atom bomb in 1945, Russia in 1949; the USA produced nuclear submarines in 1956, Russia in 1962; the USA produced muliple warheads in 1964, Russia in 1972.

The nuclear arms race has led us to a situation unique in the history of the world. Even many of those firmly committed to the doctrine of nuclear deterrence cannot fail to recognize the irrational absurdity of piling up weapons long beyond the point when either side could destroy the other. Indeed, with a global arsenal of more than 50,000 nuclear warheads the world itself could be destroyed many times over. The latest revelations about the prospect of a 'nuclear winter' in the wake of an all-out nuclear exchange add a new dimension of horror to the monstrous possibilities which might lie in the future.

Although much publicity has been given to the super-power arms talks in Geneva, an examination of the facts shows that they have so far had no impact on the nuclear build-up. Indeed, both sides are expanding and enhancing each of the three legs of their strategic triad – that is, land-based missiles, submarine-launched missiles and long-range bombers. This is probably the first time that such expansion has been taking place simultaneously in all three fields. Moreover there is talk now of the possibility of winning a limited nuclear war, and the production of the sort of tactical weapons that it is supposed would make this possible.

An American initiative

As if all that were not cause enough for grave concern, we are now faced with America's Strategic Defence Initiative (SDI), popularly and misleadingly referred to as 'Star Wars'. In a speech on 23 March 1983 President Reagan announced SDI as a project which 'holds the promise of changing the course of history'. He called the American scientific community to 'turn their great talents . . . to the cause of mankind and world peace, to give us the means of rendering . . . nuclear weapons impotent and obsolete'. This defensive shield, employing the latest technology, would, it is claimed, destroy all nuclear weapons in space before they reached their target. The

President even said that the Americans would offer the system to the Soviet Union so that both sides could be safe. The whole speech appeared to be full of moral fervour. The SDI proposals would mean an end to the immoral policy of 'mutual assured destruction'. 'Wouldn't it be better to save lives than avenge them?' Mr Reagan asked.

This speech must be reckoned as one of the most extraordinary utterances of the century and, I believe, one of the most irresponsible. It launched the most expensive research programme in history. Work on missile defence systems has, of course, been going on for some time both in America and Russia, but here was an enormous drive to remove the danger of nuclear war, not by removing the weapons, not by tackling the causes of international tension, but by building a defensive umbrella.

The British Prime Minister visited President Reagan to discuss SDI. They agreed four points:

1. The US and Western aim is not to achieve superiority but to maintain balance, taking account of Soviet developments.
2. SDI-related deployment would, in view of treaty obligations, have to be a matter of negotiation.
3. The overall aim is to enhance, not undercut deterrence.
4. East/West negotiation should aim to achieve security with reduced levels of offensive systems on both sides.

These are fine words, but doubts about SDI are voiced on all sides. Sir Geoffrey Howe, in a speech on 15 March 1985, full of reservations, said: 'The history of weapons development and the strategic balance shows only too clearly that research into new weapons and study of their strategic implications must go hand in hand. Otherwi research may acquire an unstoppable momentum of its own.' And of course it will. Already our own government sees the prospect of fat contracts and seeks for a share in the great spending bonanza which the pursuit of SDI entails. Here again we encounter the enormous power of vested interests.

The British Foreign Secretary in his speech raised the basic question which is being asked everywhere: 'Would the supposed technology actually work?' The judgment I have heard repeatedly from technical experts is: 'Almost certainly not; at least not with complete effectiveness.' It surely stands to reason that since the whole history of military advance has been a story of measures and the attempt to produce effective counter-measures, that process will continue.

In SDI, in spite of all the moralistic clap-trap used to support it, we have the latest example of the desire for military domination by seizing the high ground. All over the world there are the ruins of castles and other military installations built on the top of the highest hills. Now the USA contemplates a bid for the highest ground of all – outer space. The result of this much-publicized initiative will be a further escalation of the arms race, the inhibiting of arms control negotiations, the pouring of further astronomical sums of money into the bottomless pit of military folly, and the destabilization of the international situation. The meeting in November 1985 of Mr Reagan and Mr Gorbachov was a welcome indication of the willingness of the two leaders to do what is the obviously sensible thing – meet and talk. But SDI could prove the factor that wrecks hopes of real progress towards arms limitation.

Signs of hope

This brief attempt to examine one of the most sinister aspects of man's sinful disobedience has resulted in the painting of a dark scenario. Is there any hope? I find hope in the fact that increasing numbers of people the world over are rebelling against the folly of escalating rearmament. Elsewhere I have argued that Christians must be in the van of the peace movement and involved in the detailed debate about how the international atmosphere can be changed and the drift towards disaster halted.[1] I do not propose to repeat any of that here. I commend to those who wish to be associated with a campaign based on carefully defined objectives the World Peace Action Programme of the World Disarmament Campaign (UK). This was launched at a public meeting in the Westminster Central Hall in London on 19 November 1985. It has been supported by peace organizations and distinguished individuals in many parts of the world. It lists a series of multilateral, bilateral and unilateral initiatives for which we should be pressing, and sets them out under four headings:

1. For the prevention of nuclear war.
2. For the improvement of East/West relations.
3. For resolving world problems and strengthening the UN.
4. For disarmaments and development.

There are, however, three pre-requisites of individual commitment to peace-making which for Christians are of the greatest importance and to these I must now refer.

The first is a willingness to think theologically. Much Christian discussion of peace issues seems to be totally unrelated to the Bible and to Christian theology. In particular the doctrine of nuclear deterrence must be subjected to rigorous critical scrutiny. That doctrine rests on the belief that the only way to prevent war is to make its consequences so horrendous that no government would take the risk of initiating a conflict in which nuclear weapons would be used in retaliation. That doctrine is increasingly under fire from military experts who are themselves doubtful about its validity. The following points are frequently expounded:

1. For the doctrine to work the leaders of a potential aggressor state must be rational people able to understand the theory and appreciate the risks involved. Readers of history may doubt the rationality of many national leaders. Moreover, rational men take irrational risks and make serious miscalculations under pressure. The evidence of mental instability among personnel with responsibility for nuclear weapons is not reassuring.

2. The more complex the weaponry becomes, the greater the danger of technical error and malfunction.

3. The change of thinking from 'mutual assured destruction' to 'flexible response' and the notion that a nuclear war could be won is destabilizing. A nuclear war which started with smaller weapons would almost certainly escalate to the point where the larger weapons were used, precipitating the final disaster.

4. The danger of nuclear proliferation increases. The protagonists of nuclear deterrence often argue as if the only nations involved are the USA and the USSR. That is a very limited view in the light of the danger of proliferation.

It is necessary for the Christian to listen carefully to these practical objections, since moral judgments are not made in a vacuum. But he must go further and set the facts of the situation within the context of Christian theology and morality. One important part of that exercise must be to ask how the use of nuclear weapons can be justified by appeal to the traditional Christian doctrine of the Just War. The short answer is that it can't. The Just War doctrine has always been one of limitation. It has allowed that the use of military force may sometimes be justified, if the cause is a just one. But the means of achieving victory must always be proportionate to the end being sought. There must, for example, be reasonable assurance that the harm done by going to war will be less than that which would result from failure to defend the nation attacked against the aggressor. There must be no deliberate killing of non-combatants.

It is quite clear that the use of nuclear weapons is ruled out by the requirements of the Just War doctrine.

Then what of the argument that nevertheless the possession and threat of nuclear weapons is justified? That line of thinking fails to take note of the destabilizing effect of ever-increasing nuclear weaponry and the lack of certainty that deterrence will work. It also obscures the general understanding that if a thing is wrong in execution, it is wrong also to threaten to do it. That consideration cannot be avoided by the pretence that the threat is only a bluff. That attitude would be morally dubious even if it represented the way things actually are. In fact, there is no point in threatening to use nuclear weapons unless as a last resort you are prepared to use them. It is necessary to remember that the British Government has not been prepared to agree on a policy of no *first* use.

I was invited to give evidence to the 1985 tribunal arranged by Lawyers Against Nuclear Weapons. It met for four days and was designed to examine the question whether the possession and use of nuclear weapons are contrary to international law. After hearing a wide range of opinions the tribunal issued the following interim judgment (its full report will be published in 1986):

> The Tribunal was satisfied that the current and planned weapons developments, strategies, and deployments violate the basic rules and principles of international law both customary and conventional. The procurement and use of such weapons involve infringements of the Charter of the United Nations, the Hague Conventions of 1899 and 1907 on the Law of War, the Geneva Protocols of 1977.
>
> The evidence was convincing that the Principles of the Nuremburg Judgement unanimously endorsed by a resolution of the United Nations General Assembly as well as the Genocide Convention are being violated in the most extreme fashion by ongoing preparation to wage nuclear war, especially to the extent that plans include indiscriminate, poisonous and massive destruction of civilian populations, amounting to a conspiracy to wage aggressive war. It appears to the Tribunal that this is particularly true of newly-developed and highly accurate weapons.

The second of three requisites of individual peace-making is persistent prayer, and this for two reasons. Every time we pray for peace we are asserting our belief that peace is possible and that it is the will of God. The other reason why we must keep on praying is that we need those personal resources which will enable us to be peace-full persons. They are the gift of God. The importance of this is in inverse proportion to the space given to it.

The final pre-requisite of individual commitment to peace-making is a deep moral conviction that the existing state of affairs is intolerable. I began this chapter by referring to the sinfulness of the trade in arms. I am appealing again now for the spirit of prophetic protest against the evil of a trade which aids and abets the attitudes and policies which make for war and inhibits clear thinking and constructive efforts to build the structures of peace. 'A voice says Cry', and the response is a growing volume of righteous protest all over the world. We each have one voice to add to that global chorus.

5 | *The Divisiveness of Privilege*

We hold these truths to be self-evident, that all men are created equal
. . . *The American Declaration of Independence.*

The Bible challenges privilege

In the quiet and picturesque Cotswold village of Burford, where I
have preached on many occasions, stands the old parish church. It
would be difficult to imagine a more peaceful spot. Consider,
however, a scene from the seventeenth century. Twelve men and
nine women are kneeling throughout Sunday morning service with
heavy faggots of wood on their shoulders. Divine worship being
ended they are taken out of the church, the faggots are used to build
a fire into which branding irons are put. The twenty-one offenders
are then each branded on the cheek. What was the nature of their
offence? It was this: the leader of the group had purchased a Bible
for £1 and had been found reading it to his fellow-Christians.

The reason for this extraordinary and reprehensible action by
those in authority was that the Bible was proving to be a dangerous
book. It inspired the Levellers in their propaganda for a more
egalitarian society. These radical Christians constantly appealed to
the Bible in support of views regarded by the establishment as
outrageous. The following quotation from a Leveller pamphlet is
typical:

> The relation of Master and Servant has no ground in the New
> Testament; in Christ there is neither bond nor free. Ranks such
> as those of the peerage and gentry are 'ethnical and heathenish
> distinctions'. There is no ground in nature or Scripture why one
> man should have £1000 per annum, another not £1. The common
> people have been kept under blindness and ignorance, and have
> remained servants and slaves to the nobility and gentry. But God
> hath now opened their eyes and discovered unto them their
> Christian liberty.[1]

The long history of the human race provides us with a great variety of examples of how societies have organized their corporate life. Necessarily it also tells us much about power, for power is essential if anything at all is to be achieved. Men use power to subdue nature and produce the fruits of the earth. They exercise power to create order and structure in society. Unhappily the human story is also a sustained commentary on the abuse of power. The possession of wealth is one of the most obvious keys to the exercise of power. In every age the rich have oppressed the poor, and those in positions of privilege have exploited their fellows.

In the mid-1970s the British Council of Churches embarked on an ambitious project under the title *Britain Today and Tomorrow*. A series of working parties studied aspects of life in this country, one of these being the issue of 'Power and Powerlessness'. The conclusion was that though in Britain power is more widely shared than in many other countries, it needs to be more broadly distributed; moreover, the abuse of power is widespread. The Working Party report states:

> In Britain the 'top people' tend to be linked by education in the independent sector and, to a surprising extent, by intermarriage – a by-product in part but not entirely of our endemic class-stratification . . . There are certainly some grounds for seeing Britain today as a federation of interacting institutions, many of which are headed by people whom personal wealth, family background and education make sympathetic to each other but arguably not enough to the feelings of the majority of citizens.

The abuse of power is manifest in all sorts of situations. There is 'the insolence of office'. Politicians can become arrogant and petty officials too big for their shoes. Most of us have been occasionally outraged by overhearing some bullying clerk, corrupted by a little power, berating an inoffensive citizen who has made a perfectly proper request for information about his rights. Another example of misused power is the fomenting of violence by pressure groups, by organizations like the IRA and the National Front. The use of such violence does not change the system but it corrupts those who indulge in it. Yet another example is the power exercised by the advertisers, which tends to perpetuate the bases of power like consumerism and status.

The problems of creating a 'just, sustainable and participatory' society are formidable and have to be tackled on many fronts. There is something inspiring and moving about the ringing words in the American Declaration of Independence issued by the Congress on 4 July 1776:

We hold these Truths to be self-evident, that all Men are created equal, that they are endowed by their Creator with certain inalienable Rights, that among these are Life, Liberty and the Pursuit of Happiness. That to secure these Rights, Governments are instituted among Men deriving their just Powers from the Consent of the Governed.

It is all very well, however, to assert that 'all Men are created equal'. That is indeed God's intention. But his will is thwarted in a myriad ways and what is very apparent is that men are very unequal. The brief chapters of this book are all about this ineluctable fact. The Christian cannot escape from the imperative to seek to remove the injustices that arise because of the abuse of power and the divisions that result from the existence of the privileged and the under-privileged side by side in the same world.

Response to that divine imperative involves us in the political debate. The BCC Working Party raised some of the questions to which Christians must address themselves. They include:

How can participatory democracy be reconciled with efficient central planning?

What are the best levels for different sorts of decisions (the devolution issue)?

How can understanding between government and electorate be maximised in a highly technical society?

The Working Party went on to suggest some of the steps to be taken. These emphasize the need for positive discrimination in favour of the powerless, for example women and blacks; the encouragement of electoral reform and devolution measures designed to enable more people determine their own lives; and an emphasis on participatory democracy in the education programmes of the schools. The Report honestly acknowledges the need of the churches to examine their own life. Church leaders can scarcely be expected to get a hearing on questions of privilege if they speak out of a situation where too much power is concentrated in the hands of a minority, the clergy, and there is discrimination against a majority, the women (still in the Roman and Anglican Churches in Britain banned from the ordained ministry and, to a large extent, not involved in the machinery of ecclesiastical government).

Having raised the issue of privilege and the abuse of power in a general way, I want now to look at two areas of our national life which are of profound importance both for the individual and for the whole nation: health and education. In both of these there is a tension between the need to provide a service of excellence for all, and the ability of the privileged to ensure superior facilities for themselves because of wealth and status. This tension is one of the marks of a divided society.

Health

The Bible leaves us in no doubt that health is God's will for all his children. There are some words that cannot be adequately translated into a single word in another language. The lovely Hebrew word *shalom* is an example. It is often translated as 'peace' but it is a word which embraces the concept of wholeness, total well-being, the healthy integration of all the constituent parts of a person. The ministry of healing was a vital part of the total ministry of our Lord. The question put by our Lord to the sick man at the pool of Bethesda was typical of his approach: 'Wouldest thou be made whole?' (John 5.6).

The church at its best has always seen itself as a healing community. What that has meant in practice has varied from place to place and from age to age. The ministry of healing takes many forms. I am not here concerned with all the aspects of that many-sided ministry, but with the general concern of the church for the health of the whole community and particularly with the fact that a great deal of sickness has a societary origin. The science of epidemiology is able to draw maps of illness just as back in the 1950s Josué de Castro drew maps of hunger.[2] As I mentioned in Chapter 3, when I worked in the mining valleys of South Wales I found myself often at the bedsides of men suffering from the miner's disease, silicosis. To watch them struggling for breath as the result of dust-encased lungs was a pitiable sight.

Many of the social evils to which this book refers, like poverty and unemployment, produce their own fearful effects in the shape of anxiety neuroses, depressive illnesses, physical maladies, suicides and death. R. H. Tawney may have stated the matter too boldly when he said that 'health is a purchasable commodity', but he was surely right to underline the importance to health of political decisions. To refer to the subject of the previous chapter, the British Government can decide to spend hundreds of millions of pounds on improved health care, and thereby save thousands of lives; or it can spend even larger sums on the Trident system of defence, thus, as I would argue, increasing the insecurity of us all. It is a political

67

decision and one which has far-reaching implications for the health of the nation.

One of the greatest achievements of Britain in this present century is to bring a reasonable standard of medical care within the reach of everyone through the creation of the National Health Service, or at least to attempt to do so. We who enjoy its benefits do not perhaps always realize how vast are the strides that have been made. The followers of John Wesley sometimes express amusement at their founder's involvement with popular medicine. Some of the cures prescribed in his *Primitive Physic* sound worse than the complaint. His electric shock machine for the treatment of nervous disorders can still be seen in his tall narrow house on London's City Road. Compared with the modern equipment of today it looks rather like a penny-farthing bicycle set alongside a Rolls-Royce motor car. When he fell off his horse – which he seemed to do with extraordinary frequency – he treated his bruises with a treacle poultice.

We can, however, come much nearer to our own time to highlight the spectacular advances in medical care. In the year that I was conceived (1918) a thousand babies died every week in Britain. It was, in fact, safer to be a soldier on the Western Front at that time than to be a baby in this country. For every nine soldiers killed, twelve babies died in Britain within the first year of life. It was this dreadful state of affairs that provided the impetus for improved health services. It also played a significant part in the rise of the Labour movement.

The impact of health on politics dates back to the industrial revolution. At the beginning of the last century there was a massive migration from the rural areas into the cities. During the 1820s, for example, Bradford increased its population by 78% and West Bromwich by 60%. The houses in which these new urban workers were settled were often of the poorest quality, huddled together near the grimy factories they served, and lacking both clean drinking water and adequate sanitation. The death rate in the towns began to rise alarmingly. The killer diseases, like tuberculosis, typhus and diptheria, exacted a fearful toll.

All sections of the community were affected by epidemic diseases, but there was a marked difference between the death rate among the upper middle class and the working class. In the early part of the nineteenth century, for example, the average age of death in Manchester was thirty-eight for the former and seventeen for the latter. It was among the poor people that tuberculosis numbered its victims in thousands. Cholera, however, was no respecter of class, because it was carried through the water supply that served the whole community. It was this fact that led to the passing of the Cholera Prevention Act of 1832 and the beginning of the Public Health movement. It is unlikely that this measure would have been enacted so soon had the effects of cholera been limited to the poor sections of the community alone. Through the rest of the century the increasing concern about health and the growing awareness of the social threats to it were reflected in a series of parliamentary measures. Even so, the legislation was limited in effect and benefitted the rich far more than it did the poor. The practice of medicine itself remained at a fairly primitive level and surgery was a crude and bloody business.

A number of friendly societies and similar organizations came into being to collect money from working class families so that they might receive benefits and medical treatment at times of sickness. The idea was also taken up by the trade unions.

The first National Health Insurance Act was set up by the Liberal government in 1911. This introduced the so-called 'Panel System'. Employed men and women could receive 'free' medical treatment. The scheme was funded by the NHI contributions of the workers. Its provisions were modest and patchy, and the motives of Lloyd George's administration were mixed. They had to do something to curb the growing political power of the Labour movement; there was also a concern to improve the health of those who would presently be conscripted to fight in the war against Germany.

During and after the First World War demands for reform grew. The trade unions and the women's organizations were foremost in the agitations to provide a more effective health service which would remove the scandalous discrepancies between the benefits enjoyed by a the rich and the quite inadequate ones available to the poor.

The period of the Second World War saw a further increase in the pressure for a comprehensive National Health Service run by the State. The creation of such a service was envisaged in the Beveridge Report of 1942. The Trades Union Congress had for a long time been opposed to the policy of the insurance companies that administered the NHI scheme. The companies encouraged applicants for industrial injury benefits to opt for a lump sum payment rather than for long-term grants. Their motive in doing so was entirely commercial. The TUC wanted the matter of benefit payments to be under some kind of neutral control.

The National Health Service which began to operate in 1948 came at the end of a long period of difficult negotiations presided over by the then Minister of Health, Aneurin Bevan. He had to try to reconcile many conflicting interests. In the end the Service was largely shaped by the medical profession with its own interests very much to the fore. Those to the left of the Labour Party wanted a far more thorough degree of state control. However, general practitioners did not become salaried employees of the NHS but independent contractors to it. Consultants were offered a new hospital system paid for by the government but over which they exercised control and within which they could continue private practice.

From the beginning there has been a two-tier structure, private and public medicine, within the NHS. The Conservative party has encouraged the growth of the private sector which, of course, can only be afforded by the better-off, and Labour has opposed this, at least in its public propaganda, as an unpalatable example of class privilege. In fact the health provisions have always been better and more adequately funded in the affluent areas than in the poorer ones. The medical world is hierarchical in structure and the inequalities in the NHS reflect the unequal distribution of power within the profession itself. The highest paid members of the profession are the 'experts' and they dominate the policy-making.

In the early 1970s the Labour Party vigorously attacked the arrangement whereby pay-beds in NHS hospitals were heavily subsidized. It was estimated that in 1974 these subsidies exceeded £21 million. In fact, however, the creation by the Labour government of the Health Services Board strengthened the private sector. Under the Board the number of pay-beds in hospitals was reduced, but under an agreement whereby every pay-bed absorbed into the NHS was replaced by a bed in a local private hospital. Provident Associations like BUPA made rapid strides by presenting health insurance to the unions as a valuable bargaining counter in local negotiations. Thousands of new subscribers were recruited and private medicine grew rapidly.

The policy of Mrs Thatcher's government has been to weaken the power of the trade unions and to strengthen professional organizations. Increasingly our medical services are influenced by the market concept. The patient is the customer, the doctor is the tradesman, and he is under pressure from sundry suppliers like the drugs industry. This booming industry spends tens of millions of pounds annually on advertising, and medical practitioners are under constant bombardment. In 1979 doctors issued 370 million prescriptions for medicines costing £750 million. The profits on those sales totalled £125 million. Some drugs companies show a profit of around 30%, which is nearly twice the rate for manufacturing industry as a whole. The *Daily Telegraph* of 27 November 1979 contained the following instructive comment: 'Millions of pounds annually are added needlessly to the NHS drugs bill by mass prescribing of expensive brand-named tablets which are available more cheaply under other names.' Fortunately the Government is taking some action in the direction of ending this exploitation.

The influence of commercialism is also to be seen in the development of very costly, highly sophisticated machines and techniques which are manufactured for profit but which can only bring relief to the few who can afford the treatment prescribed. In the meantime candidates for the simpler and necessary treatment have to languish on long waiting lists.

As we look to the future there are a number of considerations which need to be given priority. There will need to be much greater emphasis on health care and the prevention of illness. As *The Black Report*[3] argued, the elimination of poverty is a vital factor in the promotion of health. The report's suggestion that reduction of wealth differentials is essential obviously goes against the grain of those who believe in the private pursuit of profit. The report takes the view that the needs of the nation can only be met by the development of community-based services at the expense of the growth of the hospital sector. These, and other proposals, raise far-reaching questions, many of which involve decisions of a political nature. The churches have a special concern for health and, as we noted earlier, their interest in healing goes right back to the Great Physician who is in all things their exemplar. But they must not confine their attention to the more pastoral aspects of healing, important as they are. They must be involved in the politics of health and the continuing debate about policies and priorities. This attempt to encourage participatory democracy will inevitably arouse controversy. The guiding principle for Christians must be the claim that health, and the services which enhance it, should be the privilege of all, and not the special possession of those who can afford them.

Education

If the churches have a special concern about health, they are no less committed to education. Jesus was not only known as the Great Healer; he was also the Great Teacher. The church has a long tradition of scholarly leadership. It founded many of the world's great centres of learning. Many of the pioneers of modern science, from Copernicus onwards, were Christians. John Wesley read widely in the scientific literature of his day. 'How well,' he exclaimed, 'do philosophy (science) and religion agree in a man of sound understanding.'[4] He believed devoutly that this 'sound understanding' required not only the influence of religion but also of education. He himself established the Kingswood School in Bath; he also founded or supported several other schools. True to this tradition Christian missionaries established schools and colleges in many countries, especially in Africa. Many of the leading figures in that Continent received their education in Christian schools.

From one point of view, however, the history of the church's involvement in education is an ambivalent one. Education has always been a source of power. In the past the clergy, many of whom were well-educated, exercised power over the local community purely because of their privileged access to learning denied to the often illiterate parishioners to whom they ministered. Speaking of the state church J. Wesley Bready says: '(it) was the most extensive, the most jealous and the most assuming of all the privileged "chartered companies" of the eighteenth century'.[5] Dr Bready describes six separate and distinct stages whereby England advanced to the point where education was available to all. They are represented by the Sunday School Movement, the Royal Lancastrian Institution (later the British and Foreign Bible Society), the National School Society, the Factory Schools, the Ragged School Union, and finally the famous Board School Act of 1870 which, supplemented by the Acts of 1876 and 1880, established compulsory education for all throughout the land.

In these great endeavours to bring education within the reach of all, many individual Christians played a decisive part. Robert Raikes, Hannah Ball, Lord Shaftesbury, Joseph Lancaster and Dr Barnardo are only a few in the long list of illustrious reformers who played their differing parts in a mighty movement.

While the temptation to linger on the details of a fascinating story is great, my main concern is to ask where the church should stand today on an issue which is still hotly debated: that of private versus public education. Once again it is an issue that tends to be politically divisive.

R. S. Tawney said: 'The idea that differences of educational opportunity among children should depend upon differences in wealth among parents is a barbarity.' Nevertheless they do. There are 259 private schools in this country registered with the Department of Education and Science. Although many of them were established to help children of the poor, they now mainly cater for the offspring of well-off parents who can afford to pay the fees, which can be in the region of £6,000 p.a. Eton College is a good example. Founded by Henry VI in 1440 as a school for boys from poor homes, it now provides education for a privileged élite. Many of these schools receive large subsidies from charitable trusts originally intended for the education of the poor. They also qualify for tax and rate relief by virtue of their charitable status. Most of them are for boys and most of them are in the affluent South of England (the North/South divide has a domestic as well as a global connotation).

Until 1975 there were 174 direct grant schools. These fee-paying schools, administered by voluntary bodies, on the passing of the 1902 Education Act became eligible for grants from central government. Under the Act of 1944 these schools had to offer free places to at least 25% of their pupils. 119 of the direct grant schools decided to become independent and join the private sector.

All of these private schools serve only a tiny proportion of the school population: less than 6%. Some of the schools have a high reputation for excellence. Many others, however, rely on the response of those who live by the philosophy that 'bought is best'.

It is possible to make out a strong case against the private schools. They enshrine privilege for the few at the expense of the rest. If one examines the educational record of those serving in the top echelons of the sectors which wield power, it will be clear that the payment of expensive school fees buys more than a good education; it secures an entry into the circles of a privileged élite whose wealth ensures power and whose power ensures wealth. A large percentage of the members of the present Cabinet at Westminster were educated in Eton or one of the other private schools (oddly usually referred to as 'public schools'). More than 200 of the 339 Conservative MPs elected in 1979 were also from that same educational background.

According to a 1973 survey the percentage of those educated in private schools now working in various powerful professions was as follow:

Upper-grade civil servants	62%
Ambassadors	82.5%
High Court and senior judges	80%
High ranking naval officers	89%
High ranking army officers	86%
High ranking RAF officers	62.5%
Church of England bishops	67% (in 1950 the figure was 74.5%)

One of the unfortunate consequences of exposure to the ethos of many of the private schools is the production of a certain sense of effortless superiority among those who easily assume that they were born to rule. The assumption is that the rest of the community were born to be ruled over. This attitude perpetuates the nastiest elements of a class system which is the enemy of attempts to achieve a participatory democracy in which all are given a chance to develop their full potential. I recall my Rhondda days and some of the characters who enriched my life and thought. They had spent a lifetime in the pits and had struggled to educate themselves by reading the big books. Given the chance they could have occupied the highest posts in the land.

Those who defend the private school system often point to the superior academic attainments of those who are able to enjoy this privileged education. But many of those schools accept pupils on the basis of academic attainment, they cream off the brightest young people, and so it is not surprising that their record appears to be superior to that of other schools. Moreover, a much higher proportion of pupils in private schools are able to remain in school beyond the age of sixteen than is the case with the children of less well-off parents.

This creaming-off of the more able by the private schools is bound to have a detrimental effect on the schools in the maintained sector which must necessarily have a higher proportion of less able pupils. Mr Mark Carlisle claimed that the private schools provide 'the maintained sector with a standard of performance as well as having traditional excellence in various fields, from which the maintained sector could usefully draw'. Statements such as that imply a denigration of state education which can only be harmful.

The 1980 Education Act introduced an Assisted Places Scheme which restores the direct grant principle which Labour abolished. The Conservative Manifesto stated that 'less well-off parents will be able to claim part or all of the fees at certain schools from a special government fund'. This scheme is open to the objection that taxpayers' money is being used to support the small private sector of privileged education at a time when the state schools are being pinched by cuts which result in shortage of equipment, reduced services and other penalties. Moreover, most of the children benefitting from the grants will come from already advantaged families.

The supporters of the private school system make much of the fact that it provides 'freedom of choice'. That freedom, however, is limited to a small minority of those who are able to afford the fees.

Those who belong to that small minority sometimes say 'why shouldn't I spend my money on my children's education if I want to? After all, I've worked hard for it, I'm not spending it on myself, and it is surely not an unworthy ambition for parents to want to do the very best that can be done for their children.' In all fairness one can only admire the often sacrificial efforts of some parents to secure the very best for their children. That fact, however, must not obscure the need to develop the state education system to provide a wider diversity of opportunities and to encourage the fuller participation of parents in the running of the schools.

The future of the private schools is an issue on which, understandably, there is sharp division between the two major political parties. As has been indicated, the Conservatives seek to strengthen the private sector and will continue to do so. Labour's policy was stated in its 1979 election manifesto. It is to 'end as soon as possible fee-paying in such schools, while safeguarding schools for the handicapped', and to 'end as soon as possible the remaining subsidies and public support to independent schools'. Needless to say, there is powerful opposition to such changes and even with the return of a Labour government progress is likely to be slow.

The Methodist Church, like the other churches, has been deeply involved in the debate about private education. It is no mere academic debate for Methodists because, in fact, their church is responsible for the running of a number of independent schools, like the one at Kingswood. Far and away the greatest part of Methodism's contribution to education is in the public sector, through the devoted service of Methodist teachers and administrators. But Methodism has defended its provision of fee-paying schools on the ground that they maintain a standard of excellence; that they enshrine Christian values which might not be upheld in state schools if some future government should terminate the present partnership between church and state; and that it is desirable to maintain variety and diversity within the educational system.

In 1977 the Methodist Conference adopted a report which examined these issues. The following excerpt summarizes its main conclusions:

On the principles outlined above the Church is certainly required to encourage and train men and women to take an active and competent part in national education at every level and in every form, as it has always done. But more than this is also required: if Christian principles are to exert any positive influence on the life of the nation they must also be embodied in the actual life of school communities. Such communities must be free from state control; maintain the highest academic and educational standards; uphold Christian values in practice as well as in theory; express the Christian faith in corporate worship, and expound it and discuss it in the classroom in a spirit of openness, with a proper respect for other systems of thought and ways of life; and promote the full development of each individual within the core of the whole. Christian principles must also be embodied in the actual life of school communities in the sense that the success or failure are related to distinctively Christian insights.

This involves at the present time the retention of independent schools with a Christian tradition and a Christian corporate life. If they fail in their Christian purposes they must be reformed. But there is no case for their abolition. Without them the Christian witness to society would be impoverished and distorted.

The report goes on to discuss the anxieties expressed by many who are critical of the involvement of the church in the provision of privileged education for the few:

It is often pointed out that the present day cost of running independent schools puts their fees beyond the reach of most people in this country. This will unfortunately remain true until more funds are available for the subvention of those who cannot afford to pay the full fees. The schools' Board of Management continues to press upon the DES the need to take more seriously the question of provision for boarding education; at the same time the governing bodies of our schools constantly keep before them the need for scholarships and bursaries to meet cases of genuine need. It is a fact of life, however, that any institution has to be paid for and Church schools are no exception. It is important therefore to recognize that no moneys raised by the Methodist Church and made available to the Division of Education and Youth are directed towards the upkeep of the schools; the whole cost of administration of the schools is paid for by the schools themselves.

Resources required for the continuation of the schools are found by parents of pupils, old students of the schools, the governing bodies, charitable trusts and private individuals. The Church is therefore not financially involved (although some of its members are, and believe it to be their duty to be so involved) in the running of independent schools, except in the limited sense of partially paying for the boarding education of ministers' children who require it. The Church might wish to play a larger part in the life and work of these schools, and would in that case no doubt think it right to accept an appropriate financial responsibility.

That disparities exist in educational opportunity is an unfortunate fact, but about this several things may be said. Firstly, the maintained system itself is not free from disparities of opportunity. Secondly, 'if not everyone can have freedom of choice, then no-one should be allowed to choose' is not a valid argument. Thirdly, discussion of the morality of private education has proceeded alongside a fearsome unwillingness on the part of society in general to pay the cost of a better education for all. Fourthly, the social cachet which goes with attendance at certain schools, which is often more evident in relation to different schools within the State system than it is when 'private' and 'maintained' schools are compared, concerns the way in which society sets its own values. It must be kept separate from the specific question whether private education itself is justifiable. Nor is the charge justified that independent schools are of necessity socially divisive. No doubt those which reflect the materialistic ethics of our society rather than any form of Christian ideal are guilty of this.

But there is evidence that those conducted according to the principles emphasized above provide, in their former students, a larger proportion of people who serve the cause of social justice here and overseas than any other kind of school. A Christian school is in fact the best possible antidote to discrimination based on race, sex, denomination, nation or class, since it is based on the Christian doctrine that God has no favourites.

The report just quoted has not convinced all the critics of the church's involvement in private education. It only seeks to justify that involvement 'at the present time'. My own visits to these schools has left me in no doubt about the excellence of the training they provide. At the same time I have found my own reservations about the system sympathetically acknowledged and indeed echoed by many of those who teach in the schools.

It is, of course, undeniable that there has been 'a fearsome unwillingness on the part of society in general to pay the cost of better education for all'. But an important part of the task of the church is to engage more fully in the battle for that better education within the state system. The argument that only by maintaining its own small expensive enclaves can the church ensure a Christian influence in education is surely of limited validity in the light of the very small contribution that can be made through the few such schools within its control.

It cannot be denied that there are special needs which in a very limited degree the fee-paying schools have met. Some children need residential education because of their parents' employment at home or abroad, and for a variety of other valid reasons. That need has never been adequately met and the existing private schools could be used within the state system to supplement the existing and inadequate provisions.

The debate within the churches must and will continue. I have dealt summarily with large subjects in this chapter but it is clear from what I have written that we are not just discussing the issues of health and education in isolation from all else. The debate under both headings is about the kind of society we want, about the ways to achieve it and how to remove those basic inequalities and injustices which inhibit the creation of true community. Once again, at least for the Christian, the background to the discussion is the cry of the under-privileged who often seem to be divided from their more privileged contemporaries by a great gulf.

6 | *The Iniquity of Discrimination*

We must love one another or die (W. H. Auden)

Some words describe an action or disposition that is wholly evil. 'Torture' is one example: there is no distinction to be drawn between good torture and bad torture; all torture is evil. Other words, however, can be used to describe an action or disposition which is either good or evil. Such a word is 'discrimination'. It is good that I should be able to discriminate between truth and falsehood, between beauty and ugliness. When, however, I discriminate against an individual because she is a woman and not a man, or because he is black and not white, that is evil. The widespread practice of that kind of discrimination has caused untold misery, and lies at the heart of many of the troubles that afflict mankind today. This chapter, then, is about sexual and racial discrimination.

Sex

At the risk of drawing ribald comments from my readers I confess that I am a great lover of donkeys, those most gentle and dignified bearers of man's burdens. I therefore take the strongest exception to the song which declares:

> I called my donkey
> A horse gone wonky.

A donkey is not a defective horse.

Much more serious, however, is the suggestion that woman is a defective man. Elaine Morgan begins her study of the sexual evolution of the human race with the following paragraph:

> According to the Book of Genesis, God first created man. Woman was not only an afterthought, but an amenity. For close on two thousand years this holy scripture was believed to justify her subordination and explain her inferiority; for even as a copy she

was not a very good copy. There were differences. She was not one of his best efforts.[1]

The idea that woman is inferior to and subordinate to man has a long history. It goes back beyond the Bible into the mists of ancient times, and in more recent days it has been advanced by representatives of the new sciences. If theology played its part over many centuries in buttressing the notion of male superiority, then biology, ethology (the science of character formation) and primatology (the study of the orders of creation) have added their testimony. I believe that testimony to be false, but it has been given with a great show of authority by many who claim to wear the mantle of the 'expert'.

The Christian must be concerned with evidence of many kinds as he tries to understand the truth about the sexes and their proper relationship. The scientific disciplines have an important contribution to make to that understanding. But the Bible has its own special importance and authority for those who follow Christ, so let us turn now to the Old and New Testaments.

The task of discovering what the Bible teaches on a particular issue, not least that of the status of women and men, is far from simple. If it were just a matter of quoting a few relevant texts, then all Christians would hold the same views on the matter. Manifestly they do not. Before we can get at the truth we have to be clear about the context of particular texts; we need to recognize how words change their meaning, both with the passage of time and as they are translated into other languages; we have to grapple with the very difficult question of how we make use of the Bible in addressing the great social issues of our own day; and we have to ask what we should do when one biblical writer seems to contradict another on the same subject.

In an earlier book[2] I tried at some length to examine the origins and development of the Christian tradition on sexual matters. Here I want briefly to concentrate on three of the great central themes of the Bible which have an important bearing on the matter we are considering: creation, fall and redemption.

The Bible opens with the sublime narrative of the creation. It is a great pity that some Christians have insisted on taking it literally, thereby making it impossible for many modern people to take it seriously. The truths contained in the Genesis narrative are of the greatest importance. Truth can, of course, be conveyed through fiction as well as through factual and historical statements. In Genesis

1.27 we have perhaps the most important statement on men and women in the whole of the old Testament: 'God created man in his own image . . . male and female he created them.' Here is the assertion that God made the male and female of the human species. 'Man' is the generic title for the whole race and has no particular attribute of gender; it means man as distinct from God or the animals, not man as distinct from woman. The assertion that 'man', or humanity in its male and female forms, reflects the image of God is profoundly significant. For Christians the image of God, as we noted in Chapter 1, is trinitarian: Father, Son and Holy Spirit. That is to say, God is, mysteriously, in his own Being, a community, a unity of three-in-one. God made humanity in two forms in order that through their relationship men and women might experience that unity which in its perfection is seen in the unity of the godhead. The truth is well-stated in Dr D. Sherwin Bailey's penetrating study. He quotes with approval from Buber's famous book *I and Thou*:

> Sex in Man is more than a mere faculty or attribute – much more, certainly, than a generative or venereal phenomenon. In the race, it is a divisive factor separating humanity into two radically different yet mutually complementary elements – male and female; in the individual, it is an informing and governing principle which permeates his being to its depths, and conditions every facet of his personality and his life. Man is a 'two-fold' being, not simply in respect of the neighbour relation, but also and pre-eminently in respect of the sexual relation; and that the latter is of such a kind and quality as to constitute in a special and peculiar sense the Manward relational aspect of the *imago Dei*.[3]

There is nothing in the first chapter of Genesis which suggests the subordination of woman to man.

In the second chapter there is another and different account of the Creation. In this the woman is created out of one of Adam's ribs: a quaint detail which makes one want to know what bit of folklore was in the writer's mind when he included it. The woman was created to be the man's 'helper'. Some have suggested that this word implies an inferior status, but the Old Testament never uses the word in that sense. In fact the word (*ezer*) is mainly used with reference to God himself.

If we move on into Genesis 3, we come to the story of the Fall. Here the central theme is that the result of sinful disobedience was the spoiling of the relationship between the sexes. One of the consequences for the woman was this: 'Your husband . . . shall be your master' (Genesis 3.16). The egalitarian nature of the relationship, which was God's original intent, was distorted by sin.

The third great theme of redemption tells us how Christ came to heal and restore the relationships poisoned and fractured by sin. Galatians 3.28 refers to the qualitative difference that redemption makes to relationships: 'There is no such thing as Jew and Greek, slave and freeman, male and female; for you are all one person in Christ Jesus.' The writer does not imply, of course, that there is no difference between men and women; rather that inequalities have been erased.

This positive attitude to women as equal partners with men was exemplified in the life and ministry of Jesus himself.

The Fourth Gospel records the conversation Jesus had with a Samaritan woman at Jacob's Well (John 4.7–27), and also refers to the surprise of the disciples, occasioned no doubt partly by the fact that our Lord talked so freely with a Samaritan, but also by his treating a woman with as much consideration as if she had been a man. 'At that moment his disciples returned, and were astonished to find him talking with a woman!' (John 4.27).

St Luke, who refers especially to the place occupied by women in the gospel story, tells us that there were a number who helped Jesus during his ministry. They included Mary Magdalene, Joanna the wife of Chuza who was Herod's steward, and Susanna (Luke 8.2–3). Women, too, played an important part in the drama of the Vigil of Calvary, and the Resurrection. It is true that no women were included in the band of twelve Apostles, and presumably also the seventy (Luke 10.1) who were sent out in pairs to the towns and villages which Jesus was intending to visit were an all-male company. No conclusion, however, can be drawn from that which would be valid in the changed social conditions of our day.

In the life and teaching of Jesus, then, we find no support either for the repudiation or suspicion of sex which characterized the attitude of some later Christians, or for the persistent notion that men and women are unequal.[4]

The largest number of references to the man/woman relationship are found in the Pauline epistles. The apostle has often been vilified by those who without giving his writings careful study have written him off as a male chauvinist who taught that women should know their place, be quiet in church, and keep their hats on. There is no space here to do justice to the many texts which need to be examined if St Paul's attitude is to be thoroughly understood. No doubt there are inconsistencies in his teaching. After all, his letters were not designed to be a manual of systematic theology. His use of the concept of male headship is apt to be very irritating to readers who hold, quite rightly, strong egalitarian views. 'While every man has Christ for his Head, woman's head is man, as Christ's Head is God . . . man is the image of God, and the mirror of his glory, whereas woman reflects the glory of man. For man did not originally spring from woman, but woman was made out of man' (I Corinthians 11. 3,7–8).

This whole passage is full of difficulty. Taken as it stands it would appear to confer apostolic authority on the subordination of women to men. Closer examination of the use of the word 'head' (*kephale*), however, reveals that it is often used to denote not authority but origin. So in Colossians 1.18 we read: Christ is 'the head of the body, the church. He is its origin.' In the quotation from I Corinthians 11 referred to above Paul is obviously harking back to the Genesis story of woman being made from the rib of a man. Scientifically, as we now know, that is nonsense. In whatever manner the male of the species originated he must have been born from woman.

However, even if the meaning of headship is not as clear as might have been supposed, it is difficult not to see Paul's teaching as reflecting the cultural setting of his day. Theologians sometimes speak of 'the development of doctrine'. I believe that Christian insights today are the development of those seminal passages, such as Ephesians 5.21, where we are bidden 'Be subject to one another out of reverence for Christ'. These have a timelessness about them which transcend the limited insights which are conditioned by contemporary cultural factors.

There is no space to examine further the teaching of the Bible nor the many other contributions that have determined the beliefs and actions of society concerning the rights and relationships of men and women. What is in fact apparent is that women have been the victims of every kind of injustice and discrimination. A few recent examples which relate to the situation in Britain will make the point.

In the sphere of work, in spite of such legislation as the Equal Pay Act (1970) and the Sex Discrimination Act (1975), there are grave inequalities. Thus, while women comprise 90% of clerical workers, nurses, canteen assistants, etc., they are only 10% of all surgeons, solicitors, architects, senior civil servants, etc. In the mid–1970s, 78% of primary-school teachers were women but only 43% of the headships were filled by women. Looking right across the board the job choices and promotion prospects for women are very restricted as compared with those available to men.

In the painful matter of broken marriages it is usually the woman who suffers most. The changes in the law in 1971 led to a huge increase in the number of divorces. In 1970 there were 72,000 petitions, and by 1980 the figure was 170,000. Now in Britain between one-third and one-half of marriages end in divorce. In 1971 the number of petitions filed by men was 44,000 and by women 67,000. In 1981 the corresponding figures were 46,000 and 123,000. Obviously women are taking advantage of their enhanced freedom. Nevertheless it is usually the woman who is left with the care of the children and evidence shows that not more than a third of the husbands are still maintaining their children a year after divorce.

My father, whom I now recognize to have been a convinced feminist, used to regale me when I was a small boy with stirring tales about the suffragettes and their often dramatic adventures during the campaign to secure 'votes for women'. As a young minister I served for a time on the National Executive of the Family Planning Association. Some of the elderly women members of that association had been closely linked with the suffragettes and now they were fighting another battle: to make birth control respectable. Then came the day when *The Times* newspaper carried a leading article praising the association for its work. There was great rejoicing among the militant ladies who saw this as a sign that the battle had been won. I thought they also revealed a certain nostalgic regret that there were no more strongholds to be assailed. They need not have worried: the struggle to enable women to take their proper place in the world is not yet over; indeed, in some parts of the world it has scarcely begun.

Here, then, is yet another cause to be served. Sexual discrimination, though it has a long history, is an ugly thing. A voice says 'Cry' and I want to join my voice to the swelling volume of protest against a manifest evil. But I have to confess to a severe sense of inhibition. I am a churchman, and a special kind of churchman at that. I am an ordained minister of the church, which means, according to the doctrine of ministry which I have received, that I am the church's special representative. If I am to cry, to speak out on the subject of the liberation of women and men – for these are two sides of the same coin – I must protest against the evidences of discrimination in the church. And I do.

Any impartial observer of the Christian church is bound to register surprise that, though the majority of its members and many of its hardest workers are women, the chief posts are largely held by men. I once had the privilege of taking a woman bishop[5] (the only one in the world at that time, so far as I know) to 10, Downing Street. I said to the uniformed official who opened the door: 'This is an historic moment. It is the first time a woman bishop has stood on this step.' His response, delivered in a flat and neutral tone worthy of the famous Jeeves himself, was, 'Indeed, sir'. But it was as plain as the number on the door that he did not believe that any such entity existed: an entirely understandable response in view of the dominance of the male in all those ecclesiastical areas where the mitre and the other appurtenances of high office are on display.

The most serious example of discrimination is the exclusion of women from the ordained ministry in many of the churches. Obviously an issue which has provoked such prolonged debate among intelligent men and women must be one of considerable complexity. I recognize that differing opinions are held with great sincerity. I can only declare my deep conviction that this exclusion is wrong and my belief that the churches which still deny entry to women called of God to the ordained ministry stand, like King Canute, with the waters of inevitability lapping round their feet.

The androcentric emphasis of the church is very fully reflected in its hymns. 'Good Christian *men*, rejoice.' 'O brother *man*', and so on *ad infinitum*. Many popular hymns employ military metaphors: 'Onward Christian soldiers, marching as to war.' Since wars have been largely fought by men one imagines that this tough male imagery is offensive to many women, as it must be also to many men.

I have confessed in the Introduction to this book that the a correction of the masculine distortions in our language raises difficulties for me. The attempts to rectify the sexist language of hymns has made some of them almost unsingable. Nevertheless we must go on trying to find ways of removing what to so many is offensive language, not least because language helps to determine and sustain the attitudes which perpetuate male arrogance and discrimination.

We need to go back to the Bible, and to the life of Christ in particular, as I sought to do at the beginning of this chapter, to discover the truth of the equal standing before God of man and woman. Only then will the gospel be good news for all his children of both sexes.

During the year when I was President of the Methodist Conference (1980–81) there was serious rioting in Brixton. The morning after the disturbances I toured the area with some of the Christian workers there. Smoke was still rising from burned-out shops. There was a strange, unnatural quiet after the noise and turmoil of the night. The smell of burning hung on the air as we walked along the shabby streets where decaying buildings stood like rotten teeth. I talked with a white community policeman who loved the area and its people. He was distressed and complained bitterly that his superiors never consulted him about the problems which lay behind the unrest. I visited a number of Methodist homes and met good, respectable people who were full of dismay, but not of surprise. They all gave examples of police harrassment, but responsible leaders saw this as only one element in a complex situation in which many factors played their part. I am sure that is a wise judgment. As the incidence of violence has spread from one inner-city area to another there has been increasing emphasis by government on the issue of law and order. Obviously the maintenance of law and order is the responsibility of government, but the introduction of more repressive measures like the use of CS gas and plastic bullets is only likely to increase fear and the mistrust between police and community. Insufficient attention has been paid to the underlying causes of unrest. This was the point made by the Birmingham Methodist Synod in its comment on the Handsworth riots quoted on p. 31.

One of the potent factors in the violent unrest to which I have referred is racial prejudice and discrimination. This fact has been recognized by the British Government which in November 1985 announced plans to improve employment prospects for black youth. (As we noted earlier, in some areas the unemployment rate among them is twice the rate for their white contemporaries). The areas which have become notorious on account of riots are multiracial areas. I want now to look at the phenomenon called racism. It was briefly defined by UNESCO in a statement issued on 26th September, 1967.

Racism, namely anti-social beliefs and acts which are based on the fallacy that discriminatory inter-group relations are justifiable on biological grounds.

The World Council of Churches produced its own fuller and descriptive definition the following year. At its 1968 Uppsala

Assembly it described racism as 'a brutalizing force', and 'the major threat to the integrity of the churches'. The definition of racism was contained in four sentences:

1. Ethnocentric *pride* in one's own racial group and preference for the distinctive characteristics of that group.
2. Belief that these characteristics are fundamentally biological in nature and are thus transmitted to succeeding generations.
3. Strong negative feelings towards other groups who do not share these characteristics.
4. Policies and attitudes that discriminate against and exclude the out-group from full participation in the life of the community.

Racist discrimination is widespread and has a long history. The Bible affords many examples. When Jesus asked a Samaritan woman at Sychar to give him a drink from the well at which she was drawing water, she exclaimed with astonishment, 'What, you, a Jew, ask a drink of me, a Samaritan woman?' Then comes the parenthetical comment: 'Jews and Samaritans, it should be noted, do not use vessels in common' (John 4.9). Racial discrimination takes many forms. In Africa, for example, there have been cruel wars like the Biafran conflict in Nigeria during which tribal enmities led to bloodshed on a horrifying scale. The notion of racial superiority fuelled the malign policies of Adolf Hitler as he sought to exterminate the Jews. Far and away the most widespread form of discrimination, however, is that practised by the white minority in the world against the non-white majority.

The basis of this iniquitous injustice is a myth, a biological heresy of the most pernicious and persistent kind. It is the belief that white people are inherently superior to all others and entitled to dominate those who, not being white, are inherently inferior. This is the conviction that undergirds the monstrous policy of apartheid in South Africa, but is also implicit in lesser manifestations of prejudice in many other parts of the world.

One of the basic necessities for those who see the urgent need to combat racism is a clear grasp of the facts. The evil of deep-seated error can only be excised with the sharp sword of truth.

We begin by examining the word 'race'. We sometimes speak of 'the human race' and this particular entity is easily distinguishable from 'the feathered race' of birds. The term 'race', however, is a difficult one. The word 'species' is easier to understand. Creatures belong to the same species if they are able to breed together and produce fertile offspring. Obviously, then, men and women the world over belong to one species. But are there different 'races' within that one species? There is general agreement that humanity can be divided into three main streams known as Mongolian, Negro, and White (or Caucasian). It is clear, however, that there has been an immense amount of mixing of these streams. Any idea of 'racial purity' will not bear examination.

Another false notion is that negroid peoples are 'closer to the monkey' than others. On the assumption that humans are descended from an ape-like ancestry, there is some evidence that the whites are the oldest part of humanity and therefore go back nearest to the apes. It is difficult to establish this beyond doubt since skeletons do not always bear a label indicating the colour of the skin that once clothed them! It is possible to distinguish some 'ape-like' qualities, but these are distributed right across the human race.

Attempts to prove that different racial types have different levels of intelligence have foundered on the fact that it is the cultural background rather than inherited aptitude which is determinative. Negro children and white children perform equally well if they have the same cultural background. If either group, however, (and it is usually the blacks) has a background of cultural and environmental deprivation, they will come out badly in comparative intelligence tests.

One other matter which is often raised in discussions on the race issue is the alleged deleterious effects on offspring of marriages between members of different racial groups. Genetic mixture is said to be a bad mixture. There is not a shred of scientific evidence to support this. What is true is that the children of so-called inter-racial marriages may suffer because of the prejudices which poison the life of the community. To make this a bar to such marriages, however, is misguided and, in view of the fact that all sorts of people fall in love with each other, pointless.

The conclusion on this issue reached by E. J. B. Rose and his associates in their massive report on British Race Relations was:

> No group of men can intelligibly be said to be 'purer' than any other or innately superior to any other. What the study of anthropology impresses upon us is chiefly the diversity of human beings. Diversity does not imply superiority or inferiority. 'Superior' and 'inferior' in this context are social concepts – they are what we make of men, not what they are.[6]

If racism is rooted in a myth, as undoubtedly it is, it is an increasingly dangerous myth. One of the extraordinary facts about the Western world is its preoccupation with the dangers of the East/West confrontation. As will have been clear from Chapter 4, I do not in any way underestimate that danger, but I believe we are not sufficiently aware of the great peril that increases as a result of the division between North and South, between rich and poor. The arms being sold by the rich to the poor could be turned on those who have sold them. We need to take account of what Ronald Segal called 'the colour of Want'.[7]

There are two sets of statistics that drive home the caveat to which I have just referred: one is the evidence relating to differentials in *per capita* income, and the other the facts about population increase. They show that it is the coloured people who are the poorest section of the world's population, and it is they who are increasing in numbers fastest.

Ronald Segal disputes the cosy picture of the British Commonwealth as a happy family. It is, he suggests, more like a street with the rich residing in fine houses while the poor struggle in the gutters outside:

> If a *per capita* annual income of £170 is the frontier of wealth, only five Commonwealth countries – Canada (£570), Australia (£544), New Zealand (£452), Britain (£448) and Cyprus (£193) – have crossed it, and they encompass only 88 million people, or some 11% of the 790 million in the whole association. India, with 471 million people, has a *per capita* income of £24; Pakistan, with 106 million, one of £25; and Nigeria, with 55 million, one of £35. The overwhelming mass of the people in the Commonwealth – some 89% – are poor, and so poor as to find mere survival the proper object of hope. Moreover, wealth and want have different skins. The five countries that have crossed the economic frontier are all 'white', while with the tiny exception of Malta (342,000 people and a *per capita* income of £140), all those still behind it are 'coloured'.[8]

The actual figures quoted in this paragraph will have changed with the passage of time, but the comparisons will not have been invalidated; today indeed they would be more sharply drawn. The figures regarding population-increase show how rapidly the coloured majority is growing compared with the white minority. The increase is less than 1% a year for Europe, but in Africa and Latin America it is nearer 3%.

Ronald Segal ends his survey of the race issue with a series of penetrating questions which show the interconnectedness of so many of the matters raised in these pages:

> Is it conceivable that the whites who have ruled so long will at last see rule itself, and the survival of poverty anywhere, as a violence done to life? Is it impossible that they should provoke revolution, rather than set out to crush it; surrender much of their wealth in the perception that riches and want should not and will not long survive together; allow and protect the opportunity of men to sort out their future through sacrifice and error and discovery? Have freedom and knowledge and peace any meaning beyond the men who make and use them? And if the mass of men cannot be trusted in the end to find, in their own way, all three, what is the point of them?[9]

Where do the churches stand on the question of racism? The records have much to tell us that is profoundly disturbing and discouraging. The complicity of the church with the slave trade is an undeniable fact of history. I referred earlier (pp. 17–18) to Wesley's condemnation of slavery, but those great Christians, like Wilberforce, who worked for its abolition had behind them centuries of comparative silence on the part of the churches in the face of this iniquitous racist trade, and even active involvement in it. Consider the advice proffered to King Philip III of Spain by the Archbishop of Valencia:

> Your majesty may, without any scruple of conscience, make slaves of all the Moriscos and may put them into your own galleys or mines, or sell them to strangers. And as to their children they may all be sold at good rates here in Spain, which will be so far from being a punishment, that it will be a mercy to them; since by that means they will all become Christians . . . By the holy exercise of which piece of Justice, a great sum of money will flow into your majesty's treasury.[10]

The attitude of the churches today is very different. I do not mean by that that the churches are free of racial prejudice, far from it; but in recent years there has been a deepening awareness of the fact that racism is evil, that it is inconsistent with Christianity, and that it must be eradicated.

One of the clearest evidences of this awareness is to be seen in the adoption by the World Council of Churches of the Programme to Combat Racism (PCR). From the Council's beginning in 1948, as the records clearly show, race relations have been a constant cause of concern. Probably no single activity of the Council has provoked greater controversy than that of the PCR. It has been misrepresented and misreported repeatedly in the media. The Council has been falsely accused of supporting terrorist activities. Some of the churches have been uneasy about the support given to organizations involved in guerrilla activities and there have been resignations from the Council in protest.

It may be that aspects of the work of PCR have not been handled well, and the Council's public relations exercise has not always worked effectively. But the PCR is an important sign of Christian determination to oppose an evil which is contrary to the perceived mind and will of Christ.

In Britain, as elsewhere in the world, the Methodist Church has been staunch in its official support of the Programme. As a sign of that support it made token grants from its central funds. This brought the church into conflict with the Charity Commissioners who ruled that support of PCR did not come within the narrowly-defined legal definition of religious purposes under which the church enjoys charitable status. The Methodist Conference nonetheless encourages individual giving to the Special Fund of the PCR.

The response of the British churches to the problems caused by racial discrimination on their own doorsteps has been inadequate. It is only fair to recognize, however, the increasing commitment of the churches to the fight for justice, and the discharge of their responsibilities in multi-racial areas. Much of the work being done is well-documented.[11] Those deeply involved in this work see their task as including the need to transform the church, its attitudes and priorities.

Needless to say, South Africa is a country where the churches face a stern challenge in the shape of a regime that has enshrined racism in its institutions. There is evidence of a new and critical thinking within those parts of the Dutch Reformed Church which have sought to provide a biblical justification for the concept of apartheid. The word 'apartheid' means 'separation'. Biblical authority is sought for the notion of black inferiority in the story of Noah's curse on Canaan whose father was Ham, the youngest of Noah's sons. The word Ham means black. Noah pronounced the curse while he was in a drunken stupor and for the flimsiest of reasons (see Genesis 9.20ff.). He said, 'Cursed be Canaan, slave of slaves shall he be to his brother.' It is almost incredible that these words could be cited in support of the view that black people were ordained by a God to be the slaves of the whites.

The situation in the Methodist Church of Southern Africa is indicated in the following quotation:

> It was decided that all circuits of the Church should be racially integrated by 1987. Priority would be given to forming circuits on a geographical instead of on a racial basis. Superintendents would be appointed on a basis mainly of proximity. Three circuits were already integrated . . . In 1982 the Methodists had resolved that apartheid could not be justified on biblical or theological grounds and should be rejected as a heresy. In 1983 the conference laid down strict conditions to govern its official relationship with the three (white) Dutch Reformed Churches. Dialogue would continue only if the following matters were included on the agenda:
> the admission of black Christians to church membership and worship, and especially to Holy Communion;
> the giving of concrete support to those suffering under apartheid; and
> the rejection of apartheid in both church and state and its replacement with a social system more in accord with Christian ethics.'[12]

For the Christian the final court of appeal in this important matter must once again be the Bible. We must therefore take a brief look at the light which it sheds on the problem of race relations.

Most Christians who have any acquaintance with theological language will be familiar with the phrase 'the scandal of particularity'. It refers to the fact that God chose a particular people to be the vehicle of his redemptive mission to the whole world. It may seem to some that it was 'odd of God to choose the Jews', but he did so. It is a fact of history that the Jews forgot why they had been chosen.

They rebelled against God, they became arrogant and proud, so that the prophets pin their hopes on a faithful remnant who will be able to carry the burden of God's purpose in choosing them. Isaiah even suggests that it may be a minority of one (or possibly a tiny group) – the 'suffering servant'.

For Christians Jesus Christ is the fulfilment of that hope. He is the Messiah of whom the prophets dreamed. Through his coming a new community is brought into being.

Membership of it does not in any way depend on the accident of birth or nationality, but on the miracle of rebirth into relationship with Christ; not on ethnic blood but on the blood of him who is the saviour of all. In the stirring words of St Paul: 'God has made every race of men of one stock to inhabit the whole earth's surface' (Acts

17.26), and again: 'When anyone is united to Christ, there is a new world; the old order has gone, and a new order has already begun' (II Corinthians 5.17). This is the universal assertion echoed again and again in the hymns of Charles Wesley who refers to Jesus as 'the general Saviour of mankind', and declares:

> For all my Lord was crucified,
> For all for all my Saviour died.

If this great biblical theme is central in Christian thinking, there can be no room for any apartheid save that of separation from sin. Shortly before his untimely death on 1 January 1968 Dr Joost de Blank, who was Archbishop of Capetown from 1957 to 1963, wrote these words:

> One of the greatest dangers confronting the modern world is the 'chosen people' attitude, which believes that as a result of divine or evolutionary selection, one section of mankind is entitled to special privileges and authority over against any other. Nothing is farther from the message of the scriptural revelation which asseverates over and over again that when God chooses a people or an individual he chooses them, not for their own sakes or for any superior qualities they posses, but in order that he may use them to serve the rest of the world until all men find their essential one-ness in him. The Israelites of the Old Testament doomed themselves to destruction when they began to take their selection for granted, even believing that this was due to some merit of their own. And we may be sadly certain that the same could happen to the church, should it fail to respond first and foremost to its vocation to be a *caring* and *serving* fellowship, and it begin to think that it exists to promote its own continuance as an institution.[13]

These are timely word for Christians in all the churches. The arguments used to bolster racist attitudes can be invalidated by using the sort of scientific data to which I referred earlier in this chapter. That is an important function of education. But for the Christian racism is not only a mistaken interpretation of the evidence, it is an evil thing, an offence to the God who created us and sent his son to redeem us. The Christian, belonging as he does to a global fellowship 'gathered out of every nation and race and kindred and tongue', must see racism as a failure to grasp and fulfil God's purpose for his children. He will also be urgently aware of the perils of continued disobedience. Racism can tear apart the fabric of society, undermine security, and fill the air with the smoke of violence. It is out of the

93

ugly strife of racial conflict that a voice says 'Cry'. That cry is a call for justice and for action. A church that fails to hear that cry is deaf to the voice of God, and that deafness is fatal.

> All I have is a voice
> To undo the folded lie
> The romantic lie in the brain
> Of the sensual man in the street
> And the lie of Authority
> Whose buildings grope the sky:
> There is no such thing as the State
> And no one exists alone;
> Hunger allows no choice
> To the citizen or the police;
> We must love one another or die.[14]

Notes

Introduction

1. Colin Morris *The Word and the Words*, Epworth Press 1975, pp. 64–5.

1   A Voice that Cries

1. E. R. Norman, *Church and Society in England 1770–1970*, Clarendon Press 1976.
2. Jack Dominian, *The Capacity to Love*, Darton, Longman and Todd 1985, p. 6.
3. Stanley G. Evans, *The Social Hope of the Christian Church*, Hodder and Stoughton 1965, pp. 255–6.
4. Alvin Toffler, *Future Shock*, Pan Books 1970.
5. John Habgood, *Church and Nation in a Secular Age*, Darton, Longman and Todd 1983, p. 177.
6. Kenneth G. Greet, *The Art of Moral Judgement*, Epworth Press 1970, p. 118.

2   The Scandal of Poverty

1. David Sheppard, *Bias to the Poor*, Hodder and Stoughton 1983.
2. Barbara Ward, *Only One Earth*, Penguin Books 1972, p. 297.
3. Barbara Ward, *The Home of Man*, Penguin Books 1976, p. 294.
4. Barbara Ward, *Progress for a Small Planet*, Penguin Books 1979, p. 277.
5. *Poverty, what Poverty?*, Child Poverty Action Group 1984, p. 3.
6. John R. Atherton, *Feasible Alternatives to a Two-Nations Policy*, Oxford Institute for Church and Society.
7. *Supplementary Benefits Commission Report*, HMSO 1980.
8. *Church of England Newspaper*, September 1980.
9. *Poverty, what Poverty?*, Child Poverty Action Group 1984, p. 14.
10. Lesslie Newbigin, *The Welfare State – A Christian Perspective*. Oxford Institute for Church and Society 1975, p. 15.
11. *North-South: a Programme for Survival*, Pan Books 1981, pp. 31–2.
12. Ibid., p. 25.

3   The Disgrace of Unemployment

1. Jeremy Seabrook, *Unemployment*, Quartet Books 1982, p. 222.
2. *Unemployment: Crisis and Opportunity*, The Methodist Church Division of Social Responsibility, 1983.

3. Ibid., p. 5.
4. Ibid., p. 7.
5. Shirley Williams, *A Job to Live*, Penguin Books 1985, p. 72.
6. Keith Smith, *The British Economic Crisis*, Penguin Books 1984, p. 233.
7. The statistics are quoted from the *Bullock Report on Industrial Democracy*, 1977.
8. *Growth, Justice and Work*, Church Information Office Publishing 1985, pp. 12–13.

4   The Sin of the Arms Trade

1. Kenneth G. Greet, *The Big Sin*, Marshalls 1982.

5   The Divisiveness of Privilege

1. Christopher Hill, *The World Turned Upside Down*, Penguin 1975, p. 17.
2. Josué de Castro, *The Geography of Hunger*, Gollancz 1953.
3. *The Black Report 1980*, Report of a working party set up by the Government under the chairmanship of Sir Douglas Black, President of the Royal College of Physicians.
4. *Wesley's Journal*, 3 July 1753.
5. J. Wesley Bready, *England Before and After Wesley*, Hodder and Stoughton 1939, p. 357.

6   The Iniquity of Discrimination

1. Elaine Morgan, *The Descent of Woman*, Stein and Day, 1972, p. 1.
2. Kenneth G. Greet, *The Muutual Society*, Epworth Press 1962.
3. D. Sherwin Bailey, *The Man-Woman Relation in Christian Thought*, Longmans 1959, pp. 269–70.
4. *The Mutual Society*, pp. 15–16.
5. Bishop Marjorie Matthews of the United Methodist Church of the USA.
6. E. J. B. Rose and others, *Colour and Citizenship*, Oxford University Press 1969, pp. 40–1.
7. Ronald Segal, *The Race War*, Penguin Books 1967, pp. 411ff.
8. Ibid., p. 411.
9. Ibid., p. 446.
10. Corinne Brown, *Race Relations in a Democracy*, New York 1949, p. 42.
11. See, for example, *A Tree God Planted: Black People in British Methodism*, 1985, and *People, Churches and Multi-racial Projects*, 1984, both published by the Division of Social Responsibility of the Methodist Church.
12. *Survey of Race Relations in South Africa*, South African Institute of Race Relations 1984 – a report from the 1984 Methodist Conference held in Durban.
13. *Race: a Christian Symposium*, Gollancz 1968, p.123.
14. W. H. Auden, 'September 1, 1939', reprinted by permission of Faber from *The English Auden*, Faber 1977, p.246.